T
Marketing
Cookbook

The Winning Recipe of Ingredients for Marketing Your Business

Tom Liebrecht
Bill Kozdron

Copyright 2013

Today's Marketing Cookbook
The Winning Recipe of Ingredients for
Marketing Your Business

By: Tom Liebrecht and Bill Kozdron

Printed in the United States of America

First Printing 2013

For permission to reproduce or to order additional copies of this book, contact
Tom Liebrecht and Bill Kozdron
By sending a request to:

tliebrecht@msn.com

Dedications

I dedicate this book to my wife, Michelle. Her love, honesty and unwavering support are the cornerstone of my life.

I also dedicate this book to the people throughout the world who have the vision, creativity, courage and perseverance to launch new businesses and succeed. You are the lifeblood of a global economy and the keys to a prosperous and rewarding future for all.

Tom Liebrecht

This book is dedicated to my beautiful, amazing and always supporting wife, Sheri. Not only did she edit this book, but she's the best partner anyone could ask for. I couldn't imagine this journey without her by my side.

In addition, I'm dedicating this book to my son, Owen. I want him to realize that anything you dream can become reality. You just have to work hard and have a clear vision.

This book is also dedicated to the wonderful friends and family who support me every day and to the entrepreneurs out there who dream of finding financial freedom by living their passion.

Bill Kozdron

Acknowledgement

I want to extend a special thanks to my co-author Tom Liebrecht, who came to me with the vision of creating this book. I am so appreciative of his professionalism, support and friendship. His drive to finish this book was certainly inspiring.

Bill Kozdron

"There are no secrets to success. It is the result of preparation, hard work, and learning from failure."

Colin Powell

Disclaimers

Information and opinions related to marketing and advertising a business are subjective in nature. The contents of this book are for general educational and informational purposes only.

Every business is unique and the information contained within this book may not apply to your specific situation.

The authors provide no warranty, either expressed or implied, about the content or the accuracy of content contained herein.

The authors shall not be held liable for any loss of profit or any other types of damages resulting from the information provided within this book.

Any and all examples of results contained within this book are only examples. They are not intended to represent or guarantee that similar results can be achieved.

TABLE OF CONTENTS

Introduction: 1
A Recipe of Many Ingredients

Forward: 4
Focus on Who Will Be Eating Your Recipe,
Don't Focus on Yourself

**Three (3) Important Words to Remember
Before We Begin:**   7
Relevance, Authenticity and Authority

Ingredient 1:   12
An Efficient, Effective and Economical Website
(But It Doesn't End Here!)

Ingredient 2:   31
Know Your Keywords and the Basics of Search
Engine Optimization (SEO)

Ingredient 3:   48
Update your website monthly

Ingredient 4:   51
In-Bound links, Out-Bound Links

Ingredient 5:   57
Local Business Accounts on major
search engines of Google, BING and Yahoo

Ingredient 6:   62
Citations
(Internet Business Directory Listings)

Ingredient 7:   67
Blog

Ingredient 8:   71
Press Releases (on-line and off)

Ingredient 9:   78
Pay Per Click Campaigns on Google, Bing /Yahoo,
Facebook and LinkedIn.

Ingredient 10:   85
Email Marketing

Ingredient 11:   91
Social Media Marketing
(Facebook, Twitter, Google +, LinkedIn, Pinterest)

Ingredient 12:   100
 Videos and YouTube

Ingredient 13:   105
Go Mobile

Ingredient 14:   109
Cost Effective Direct Mail

Ingredient 15:   116
Print Advertising & Classified Ads

Ingredient 16:   **121**
Events

Ingredient 17:   **127**
Analytical Tools
(Google Analytics, Google Webmaster and More)

**Taste Testing, Evaluation and Recipe
Refinement**   **140**

Maintaining Consistency of Your Recipe   **142**

Sous-Chefs: Finding the Right Help   **144**

Authors   **148**

"There is only one boss- the customer. And he (or she) can fire everybody in the company from the chairman on down, simply by spending his (or her) money somewhere else"

Sam Walton

Introduction:

A Recipe of Many Ingredients

It's an exciting time to be marketing a business in today's world. There are a wide variety of options readily available that enable any size organization to gain visibility with its targeted audience efficiently and economically.

With all the marketing opportunities currently available and new ones routinely appearing, it can be overwhelming. Add the flood of solicitations promoting new marketing tools and it gets confusing.

The truth is a lot of the fundamental business practices and marketing principles still hold true in today's environment of never-ending options. However, it's important to realize and understand that it takes a mix of many ingredients to successfully market a business today. When you do develop the right mix of ingredients, the results will speak for themselves and you will have created a winning recipe.

You may recall the 1989 movie *Field of Dreams* with Kevin Costner and James Earl Jones. Some of the most moving scenes during the movie are the "voices" that deliver messages to the main character, Ray Kinsella. These voices inspire, motivate and compel Ray to destroy a large portion of his cornfield and build a baseball diamond. The "voice" whispers, *"If you build it, he will come."*

Ray Kinsella listens to the "voices", builds a baseball field and the ghosts of legendary baseball players from the past appear.

While the *"build it and they will come"* strategy may work in the movies, it doesn't usually work in real life. We've run into way too many businesses who believe if they build a website on the internet, the flood gates will open and people will come. That could not be further from the truth.

The internet is a very competitive and fluid environment in which to market and advertise. It takes a recipe of many ingredients to be successful and drive desired results. Creating a website is just the first step and only one of the many ingredients necessary for a successful marketing plan.

We wrote this book to help businesses become aware and understand the list of viable "ingredients" that are readily available and should be considered as a business formulates its winning recipe.

A recipe that gets the business visibility, reaches an audience the business wants to target and delivers messages that compel action. In other words, a recipe that helps a business succeed and grow.

We cover both opportunities that are available on the internet (on-line) as well as more traditional forms of marketing and advertising (off-line) that are more effective today than ever thanks, in large part, to the internet.

We sincerely hope the following pages help you better understand how to take advantage of the wonderful opportunities to market a business today as well as how to stay away from mistakes that will waste your time and money.

We've helped a long list of businesses in a diverse set of industries develop their unique mix of ingredients that created winning recipes and fueled growth in new customers, new clients, new patients and product sales.

You have the information at your fingertips in the pages that follow to find your own mix of ingredients that will lead to a winning recipe.

We wish you much success with your recipe!

Sincerely,
Tom Liebrecht and Bill Kozdron

Forward:

Focus on Who Will be Eating Your Recipe, Don't Focus on Yourself

The key to any successful recipe is to focus on who will be eating that recipe. You may like peanuts, but just because you like them doesn't mean that everybody else does. In fact, many people have peanut allergies and do everything they can to stay clear of anything remotely related to peanuts. They not only avoid the actual peanuts but also all the other types of food from factories where peanut products are manufactured. Obviously, you don't want something like that to happen to you.

Many businesses are overly focused on themselves when it comes to marketing. The Home Page of their website features a picture of their building or a picture of their staff. They run ads in the newspaper with headlines saying "We are the best". Who do they think they are marketing to?

Developing a list of ingredients that turns into a winning recipe involves focusing on the people who will be "eating" your recipe. In other words, it should identify with a problem, need or desire of your targeted audience. Talking about your business is important too, but it should not be the first message or image that someone sees. Talking about how your business can solve a problem, satisfy a need or fill a desire is the priority. Your potential clients want to know what you can do for them, how your business can solve their problem(s).

The history of your business, its people and its qualifications all play a supporting role in your marketing efforts. As you develop your winning recipe of ingredients and grow your business, your service or product should start to speak for itself in terms of satisfied customers, clients or patients. People will talk to others about your business on your behalf. That's called Referral Marketing and it's the most powerful form of marketing!

It's prudent to study, survey and take into consideration the demographics as well as the behaviors of your targeted audience. How old are they? What's their marital status? Do they have children? What are their professional and personal interests? All these types of questions should be addressed and incorporated into the development and implementation of marketing strategies and plans. If you know the answers to these types of questions, you will be able to evolve your list of ingredients into a winning recipe much faster than if you don't take the time and conduct the research.

As you read this book and begin to formulate your list of ingredients, put yourself in the shoes of your targeted customers, clients or patients. See it from their perspective and be conscious of who will be "eating" your recipe.

Three Important Words to Remember Before We Begin the Recipe:

1 - Relevance
2 - Authenticity
3 - Authority

In general, these three words play a very important role in all marketing. But when it comes to on-line marketing and ranking high on internet search engines like Google, Yahoo and BING, these three words are vital to achieving any level of success.

Internet search engines like Google are constantly refining their methods for delivering quality results for users. When they deliver quality results, people will keep using that search engine over and over again. If people are loyal to one search engine, that provides the search engine with opportunities to generate a lot of revenue. For example, it's estimated that well over 300 million people use Google (the most popular internet search engine) every day. As a result of all that use, Google is able to earn around $50 billion in revenues each year.

Your strategies for building relevance, authenticity and authority should touch everything that you do and every decision you make. This applies to your marketing, your customer service, your employees, your business culture and every other aspect of your business. It's important to understand what each of these words means.

Relevance

In the world of internet search engines, relevance means how closely something on the internet matches a user's search for information. For example, if a person is using Google to search for a local plumber because the waterline to their shower broke and water is filling up their bathroom, then Google will display search results that it thinks are the most relevant to that person's search. Obviously, you want Google to think your business or product is the most relevant.

The mix of ingredients you create for your winning recipe should be highly focused on relevance. If you are a plumber who makes emergency house calls to fix water leaks, then you need a website that states this fact. You also need listings on local internet business directories that state this fact.

If you are a supplier of plumbing parts and not a plumber who makes emergency house calls to fix waterlines, you are not relevant and should not make statements on your website that say you do those things.

Many times, websites are deceivingly built to attract as much traffic as possible regardless of whether that traffic is relevant or not. This practice is a waste of time for a visitor to a website who was not searching for the product or service and it will not lead to a good experience for that person. This is also something internet search engines like Google don't like and try to avoid. Google (and other internet search engines) are making constant refinements to make sure the results they are providing to their users are highly relevant.

Authenticity

It's very easy to be lured into the practice of duplicating what others have done. When something is successful or appears to be successful, it's tempting to want to duplicate it. After all, if something worked once, should it not work again? In the short term, duplicating what others have done may deliver results. However, it is not a good long term strategy for any business to follow. Be a leader, not a follower!

As Ralph Waldo Emerson said, "Do not go where the path may lead, go instead where there is not path and leave a trail"

When it comes to marketing a business, you need to be authentic for a long list of reasons. First and foremost, there is only one you or one business like yours. No one can duplicate your business exactly and that is a competitive advantage for your business.

If you are an auto mechanic and your competitor located a few blocks away offers 10-minute oil changes, you probably won't gain a lot of market share by advertising you also offer 10-minute oil changes. It's not authentic and it doesn't tell people what distinguishes you from your competitor down the street. If you advertise that you offer oil changes where people don't have to get out of their car, that's authentic and clearly sets you apart.

When it comes to the internet, search engines will reward your authenticity by ranking you higher in search results. If you duplicate the content of others (that's plagiarism) or even duplicate your own content, the search engines will penalize you. This includes duplicated content from free article sources. Posting free articles can and most likely will be a detriment in the long run.

Be authentic in your business. Over time, you will see the huge dividends this strategy yields.

Authority

When you look up the definition of the word authority, you will see references to power, control, high position, expertise and ability to influence. Most businesses will agree these are all qualities they want to have and the reputation they want to enjoy in their marketplace. You want your business to be seen as an authority. You want to be the expert in your field and in your marketplace.

To achieve authority it takes time, hard work, relevance and authenticity. Rarely do new businesses open their doors armed with authority. However, they can steadily build authority. Once they have established a certain level of authority, it will make their list of ingredients for a winning recipe very potent and greatly enhance the recipe.

Internet search engines factor in authority as well. Those businesses that are focused on building their authority over time will see their rankings in search engines results maximized because of their efforts. Authority is a quality that both search engines and people respond to very favorably. Because of this fact, your business should too.

When developing your list of ingredients for successfully marketing your business, keep your focus on the three words...Relevance, Authenticity and Authority. Do not waste your efforts getting distracted by others or copying what they're doing. It is simply not worth your time and not beneficial in the long run.

Keeping relevance, authenticity and authority top of mind, let's now look at the list of potential ingredients for your winning recipe.

Ingredient **1**

An Efficient, Effective and Economical Website (But It Doesn't End Here!)

In today's world, it's hard to think of a business that should not have a website. Given the rapidly growing number of internet users globally, the internet is a place nearly all businesses should want to be and a website is a great way to establish visibility on the internet.

To create a website, there are almost limitless options. You can create one yourself using an array of templates or you can hire someone to build your website for you. Whatever option you take, your website needs to look professional. It needs to be properly structured. It needs to be relevant. It needs to be authentic, and it needs to provide your target audience with the information and the elements to compel them to contact your business so they schedule an appointment or buy your product. You can accomplish all these things efficiently, effectively and economically.

Contrary to what many people think, a website does not have to be extremely sophisticated, playing introductions that look like the trailer for a summer blockbuster movie with all types of bells and whistles. In fact, simple and straightforward websites that identify with a target audience and deliver the relevant information these people are searching for will perform much better than a fancy and expensive website that fails to satisfy these requirements.

Here are the recommended elements for most business websites:

1. Company/ Business name and logo positioned in the upper left hand corner.
2. Company/ Business tag line positioned at the top.
3. Telephone number positioned in the top right hand corner.
4. One row of navigation buttons positioned under the above listed items that take you to different pages of the website.
5. Clean, simple and professional design. Avoid busy patterns, clutter and more than 3 different colors.
6. Photos.
7. Videos.
8. Contact Forms.
9. Live Chat Capability.
10. Written content prepared in a manner appealing to both website visitors (people) and internet search engines.

The written content must contain marketing messages that appeal to a website visitor's problem, need or desire and direct 'calls to action'.

11.   Search engine optimization (SEO) features. This includes items like relevant keywords, page titles, page descriptions and site maps.

The most critical pages of a business website include:

1. Home Page
2. About Us Page (Company Overview)
3. Services / Products Page (If you have different services and products, set-up a separate page for each product or service.)
4. Blog Page
5. Contact Us Page
6. Schedule an Appointment Page (for service providers like dentists, chiropractors, medical doctors, optometrists, financial planners, accountants, attorneys, etc. Make this a separate page from the Contact Us Page)
7. Location and Business Hours Page with Google Map (If you have more than one location, set-up a separate page for each location.)
8. Testimonials from Customers, Clients or Patients.
9. Special Offers Page to list special promotions, free information or coupons.

Let's take a close look at the most essential elements for most business websites.

(1). Company / Business name and logo

This element speaks for itself. Your website needs to immediately identify the name of your business and display your logo. Make sure the name and logo on your website is consistent with the way your business name and logo appears on your store or office along with all your other marketing materials. This consistency plays a big part in branding your business.

Logos must look professional. It's usually the first thing a visitor sees on your website and you've only got one chance to make a good first impression. If it's hard to read, the colors don't match, or it looks amateur, you may want to have a professional graphic designer create a new logo. It will be well worth it in the long run.

(2). Company / Business Tag Line

A tag line is an important element that many businesses overlook. In the world of the internet where the attention span of a user lasts for mere seconds, a tag line is critical in communicating with a potential customer visiting your website and sparking their interest to spend more time on your site learning about your service, your product and your company. A tag line should be short in words but make a huge impact. Over time, a well developed tag line with be as recognizable as your name and logo, if not more so.

Do you recognize any of these popular tag lines?

"Just Do It"(1)
"Don't Leave Home Without It"(2)
"The Few. The Proud"(3)

(3). Telephone Number Positioned in the Top Right Hand Corner

Over the years, website users have become accustomed with finding telephone numbers and contact information in the upper right hand corner of a website. It's what people have come to expect and what they want. Therefore, give it to them.

Another important aspect to highlight when it comes to telephone numbers is consistency. When search engines crawl your website and check your site for relevancy and authenticity when of the things they are checking is the accuracy and consistency of your business telephone number. For example, if you own a restaurant in Columbus, Ohio and your business is listed in the 411 telephone directory as (614) 555-555, your website should also list that same number, as should all other places on the internet associated with your business.

This consistency is something the search engines like. It reassures the search engines that your business is legitimate and is a great choice to deliver in the results of a search someone is conducting on that search engine for a keyword that is related to your business. In other words, the consistency of your telephone number across a variety of internet sources helps you rank high in search engines results.

(4). Clear and Easy to Read Navigation Buttons at the Top

Just like website users expect to see telephone numbers in the upper right hand corner of a website, they also expect to see easy to read navigation buttons positioned towards the top of a website page that will take them to new pages containing the information they are looking for.

Don't make the mistake of using too many navigation buttons. A website with too many navigation buttons will quickly lose its simple and clean design. When this happens, people will get turned off and leave your site.

(5). Clean, Simple and Professional Design

The internet and websites have been around long enough to know what the majority of people like and don't like. Websites that are organized, clean and simple are far more engaging than those sites that are very busy and cluttered. People who are surfing the internet and websites are, for the most part, skimming across information. They are quickly trying to find something that captures their attention and satisfies their problem, need or desire. Keeping things organized, clean and simple is the way to go given the way people behave on the internet.

Apple (apple.com) does a great job of keeping their website's design clean, simple and engaging. Given that Apple is one of the most successful companies in the world and has one of the most visited websites on the internet, they must be doing it right. When you visit Apple's website, note the following:

1. The use and the amount of white space.

2. The position of their logo.

3. The position and number of navigation buttons.

4. The use of photos.

5. Easy to read text.

6. Clean (not cluttered) appearance.

We are not Apple nor are you. Therefore, don't copy Apple's website, just refer to it as a way to learn what an industry leader like Apple delivers to its millions of users who visit the Apple website daily.

(6). **Photos**

As the old saying goes, "*a picture is worth a thousand words*". When it comes to your website, it's worth way more than that! Simply revisit what Apple (apple.com) is doing on their website.

 What is the first thing you see when you arrive on the Apple website? Large photos of their products. These photos dominate the Apple website because they not only immediately identify with a visitor's need and/or desire, but they "say" so much to each individual website visitor without using written text, video or audio.

Your website should utilize photos and these photos should be of a high quality. We highly recommend that you use photos that are purchased from stock photography websites or hire a professional photographer to take photos that will be used specifically for your website.

Don't copy photos from other websites and others places on the internet and place them on your website. That's a copyright infringement. It's also a big deviation from one of the **Three Most Important Words** that we talked about at the beginning of this book – Authenticity.

Photos not only help to maximize the user experience on your website, they are also a tool for SEO (search engine optimization). Photos can be tagged with keywords that are relevant to your business so that search engines pick them up. Notice when you are using the Google search engine that one of the options on Google is the option for "Images".

(7). Videos

When asked if they would rather read the book or watch the movie, most people choose to watch the movie in order to save time. Video is an effective element for a website to engage visitors and get them to learn more about you, your service or your product. Today, it's easier and more economical to shoot a video than ever.
Video is a tool that enhances the time a visitor spends on your website. You can use one video or multiple videos on different topics that are positioned on different pages of your website.

There are a few very important rules to follow when featuring a video on a website. The first is the duration of the video. Always remember you are dealing with users who do not have a long span of attention. Videos should be no more than 1-2 minutes in length. In fact, the closer to 1 minute a video is in duration, the better. Given this short window of opportunity, a video needs to deliver its message quickly.

Another attractive quality about videos is that they can be utilized on video websites like YouTube. YouTube was acquired by Google in 2006 and has been turned into a very popular search engine. In fact, YouTube is the second most popular search engine. The most popular is Google. People are searching for information on YouTube much like they are searching for information on Google. The places where people search for information and answers are where you want to be.

Search engines are also looking for videos in their never ending quest to provide their users with high quality and relevant content of all kinds. Similar to photos on websites, video is also an important element for SEO. Notice when you are using the Google search engine that one of the options on Google is the option for "YouTube".

(8). **Contact Forms**

Visitors to your website need to have an easy way to contact you. The majority of people like to contact your business by calling the number listed on your website. However, your business may not be open 24 hours a day, 7 days a week. In addition, some people simply do not want to contact you via telephone. So you need to give people alternative ways to contact your business. Many people like to use a contact form located on your website. A contact form is also a great way to capture a visitor's information for future use.

Another benefit using a contact forms is they are a great way to keep all communication from your website coming from one place. In addition, they are effective at preventing spam which would be the result of just placing your email on a website.

When someone fills out a contact form on your website, the contact form should contain the following fields:

1. Name

2. Telephone Number

3. Email Address

4. Questions or Comments

(9). **Live Chat Capability**

Chat is another option people visiting a website like to utilize. In fact, it can significantly increase the number of leads or sales generated from your site. A dominate behavior for internet users is instant gratification. Thanks to Google and other search engines, think about how easy it has become to get your questions answered and your search for information quickly resolved. We simply type or speak a couple of words into Google and instantly receive results.

A live chat feature on a website matches well with the instant gratification behavior. When a website visitor wants to get in touch with you, a chat features allows them to do that quickly without having to pick-up a telephone and hoping someone will answer or worse yet, they do answer then place you on-hold.

Chat also makes the communication perfectly clear. You are reading real-time text (words) being typed by the website visitor instead of trying to battle with background noises or a bad cell phone connection.

There are a variety of options when it comes to placing a chat service on a website. You can purchase a monthly subscription which will provide you with the necessary software to handle the chats internally by one or more employees. You can also subscribe to 24 hour chat monitoring services that have operators standing by at all times to take chats from your website. You typically have the ability to provide the chat operators with scripts to follow so they know what questions to ask or how to respond to questions. The transcripts from these chat are forwarded to your business where you or your employees can follow-up with the website visitor who initiated the chat.

(10). **Written Content**

The written copy for a website requires a unique style of writing. It's a writing style that incorporates marketing messages, appeals to the behavior of people using the internet and follows the rules for search engines.

When we write content for a website, we like to start by using some readily available tools. One of the most useful is offered by Google and it's called the Google Keyword Tool (googlekeywordtool.com). The Google Keyword tool provides keyword ideas related to the topics your website pages are targeting.

For example, let's say you are a florist opening a new flower shop in Battle Creek, Michigan. You are building a new website for your florist business and want to write content for your website. You start by using the Google Keyword Tool to get ideas for keywords you should incorporate into the written content. Using the Google Keyword Tool, you type in the word "florist" and the Keyword Tool provides you with a list of keyword ideas along with information on how many searches are conducted each month for each keyword.

Here's an example:

Keyword	Local Monthly Searches
Florist	4,090,000
Florists	3,350,000
Florist delivery	246,000
Florist shop	550,000
Wedding florist	110,000

The Google Keyword Tool gives you an understanding of the keywords that are generating activity and will most likely produce activity for your website as well. Therefore, these are keywords you want to consider incorporating into your written content.

But don't just focus on keywords. As outlined above, a website's written content should be written in a style that delivers your unique message to the people that will visit your website. The writing should be conversational, easy to understand and brief.

(11). Search Engine Optimization (SEO)

Search engine optimization or SEO is very important for a website in order for the search engines to find you and rank your website so that people will find you. SEO is a moving target because search engines are constantly refining the ways they deliver their search results in order to provide users with high quality results. If you are using the Google search engine to find a grocery store that carries the spice saffron, you want to see results that show grocery stores that carry this very expensive spice that are in close proximity to you. It's Google's goal to provide you with results you can trust.

When it comes to website SEO, how you build your website and the information you include in page titles, page descriptions and keyword tags are all very important. You want to make it attractive to the search engines and easy for the search engines to identify as the most relevant, the most authentic and the highest authority.

Now that we have covered the most essential elements of a website, let's take closer look at the most critical pages of a website.

(1). **Home Page**

The Home Page of a website is your opportunity to meet a website visitor, identify with their problem, need or desire and make a good impression so they spend time on your website and ultimately contact you or purchase your product. Incorporating the essential elements outlined previously is very important for your Home Page.

Fight the urge to put everything on your homepage. Instead, try to answer this question: What do you most want the visitor to take away from your site with the little bit of time they were there?

That is the ultimate goal - the takeaway. If a visitor leaves your site and they don't remember anything after leaving then you have lost a potential customer or patient. You want to stand out and be memorable.

(2). **About Us Page**

This page provides you with the opportunity to provide additional details about your business, its history, how it started, why it's different or unique and information about the people – owners, management, employees, etc.

Original photography is important on the About Us Page. People like to see the real people behind the company. It's a great way to engage a website visitor and build a relationship.

When you write the copy for the About Us Page, write it in a style like you were having a conversation with a customer or patient face-to-face. Use words and phrase that resemble the following:

- I started this company in…

- We make sure every product we manufacture is of the highest quality….

- When you come to our store, you will be greeted with a smile…

Note the use of the words "I", "we", "you".

(3). Services / Products Pages

 Each service or product that you provide should have one website page that provides a summary of the services or products and you should also have a website page dedicated to each of the services or products. For example, if you are a dentist that offers the following services:

1. Emergency dental care

2. Check-ups

3. Fillings

4. Root canals

5. Dentures

6. Implants

7. Teeth Whitening

You should have one page of your website that lists all these different services together as well as a separate website page for each of the services listed. Therefore, the website would have a page for emergency dental care, a page for check-ups, a page for fillings, a page for root canals, etc.

(4). **Blog Page**

Blog articles are a great way to keep your website active and fresh. The search engines like website that are constantly being updated with new written content, new photos, new videos and new keywords. We recommend posting an article at least once a week, but that really depends on the company and what you are selling. Some websites will benefit from posting twice a week or even every single day.

(5). **Contact Us Page**

There should be a page to your website specifically dedicated to the various ways a visitor to your website can contact your business. The page should list your telephone number, fax number, include a contact form, have a button to engage a chat session and include written content that invites and encourages people to contact you.

(6). **Schedule an Appointment Page**

For businesses that provide services where appointments can be scheduled, create a separate page for this. This page is different from the Contact Us page. The Schedule an Appointment Page allows a website visitor to let you know they want to schedule an appointment at a certain time on a specific date. Create a separate contact form that allows a website visitor to enter all the information necessary to schedule an appointment on-line via your website.

If you can have a live scheduling program incorporated into your website that really increases appointments and reduces wasted time playing phone tag with potential customers.

Customers appreciate ease in scheduling and the convenience. You can immediately show the client all available time slots, and they can make their selection 24/7. Even for businesses that need to be able to schedule in person as well as online, many scheduling programs do both. We recommend using a program that will embed right into your site and not direct clients to the site of the scheduling system. Some even allow clients to book through social media sites, like FB.

(7.) Location and Business Hours Page with Google Map

Create a page that lists your location (address) along with your business hours. Include photos of the exterior of your store or office. Reference near-by landmarks in close proximity to your location that are easy to identify. In general make it very easy for someone to find you. Be sure to embed a Google Map on this page of your website that identifies your business location. If you have more than one location, create a separate and unique page for each location.

(8.) Testimonials from Customers, Clients or Patients

What others say about your business is extremely powerful and extremely valuable. Dedicate a separate page of your website to the testimonials from satisfied customers, clients or patients.
You need to make it a priority to ask for testimonials from customers. If you can get a photo of your customer to go along with the testimonial, that will make the impact of the testimonial even better. You can never have too many testimonials and happy customers, clients, or patients are usually very willing to give them if their experience has been good. Consider rewarding your customer for the testimonial by giving them a coupon or a gift card along with a personal and sincere "thank you".

Testimonials are not just limited to written form. Video testimonials and audio testimonials are great too. In fact, a variety of written, video and audio testimonials will make your testimonials more interesting and engaging.

It's a good idea to also add a star rating system to each of the testimonials on your website. People love star ratings and it builds trust. Google, Yelp and other popular business websites use the star rating system, so people are very accustomed to seeing this.

(9). Special Offers Page

People respond to coupons, discounts, promotions and other types of special offers. Create a separate page for your website where you can upload coupons, offer discounts and run specific promotions. When businesses have a page for special offers, it's routinely one of the most popular pages of their website. People like this!

Special offer promotions also work well with social media marketing. You can promote special offers on popular social networking sites like Facebook and Twitter and send them directly to your website.

Your website is a very important part of your marketing program. In fact, we believe it's the cornerstone of most marketing plans. Websites don't have to be overly complicated and they don't have to be extremely expensive.

Remember that once your website is built, it doesn't end there. Rather, it's just the beginning. You need to add and implement additional ingredients that will drive quality traffic to the website. The ingredients that follow will do just that!

Notes and References:

(1) This is the tag line for Nike.

(2) This is the tag line for the American Express Card.

(3) This is the tag line for the United States Marine Corps.

(4) This is the tag line for Verizon.

(5) This is the tag line for Timex.

Ingredient **2**

The Basics of Search Engine Optimization (SEO) and How to Identify Your Keywords

For most people, SEO (which is the acronym for search engine optimization) sounds mysterious and complicated. This is why most business owners are bombarded by all types of marketing and advertising information from SEO firms about how SEO will either make or break your business in today's world.

While SEO does involve many moving parts and is very detailed, it really isn't all that mysterious or complicated. In fact, a lot of plain, old-fashioned common sense and fundamentals of marketing are involved with SEO. This chapter will cover the basics of search engine optimization, help you understand SEO and show you how and why to identify the keywords associated with your business.

While SEO is important, it's only one ingredient in the many ingredients of a successful marketing recipe. By itself, it will not make or break a business. In fact, there are some businesses where spending a lot of time and resources on SEO may not make much sense at all. In general however, being effective with SEO will most likely enhance your internet marketing efforts and the overall results from your marketing program. Therefore, it is an important ingredient for marketing success.

Because the term "SEO" is thrown around so frequently and used rather loosely, let's first define it. Search engine optimization is the process of affecting the visibility of a website, a webpage, a blog article, an on-line press release, a video uploaded to the internet, a photo posted on the internet or any other type of content in a search engine's natural or organic (non-paid) rankings. The more visible your content is on a search engine (i.e. the higher the content ranks on a search engine and the more frequent it appears within search results), the more probability that piece of content will be utilized by people searching on the internet.

As highlighted above, SEO involves many different types of search. It's not just about websites and written content. SEO also targets image (photo) search, video search, local search, address search (maps), news and much more. Just look at the options on Google's Toolbar and note how they accommodate these different types of searches:

The practice of SEO involves understanding how internet search engines like Google, Bing and Yahoo work, what people are searching for on these search engines, how people are conducting their searches (keywords and keyword phrases being used) and tactics to attract and gain favor with search engines.

SEO is not stagnant by any means. It's constantly evolving because search engines are continually modifying how they rank content in order to provide the best quality results and combat those who are trying to manipulate search result rankings. In addition, people using search engines are continually changing the way they conduct searches and the keywords and keyword phrases they use to search.

So how do you keep up with all this change? One of the best things you can do is adhere to the *"Three (3) Important Words to Remember Before We Begin"* chapter of this book. Once again, those three words are (1) **Relevance** (2) **Authenticity** and (3) **Authority**. Stay true to these three rules and your response to change becomes less frequent and dramatic. For the most part, the major changes implemented by search engines are to battle manipulators and scammers who are trying to get high organic rankings by NOT being relevant, authentic or an authority. Stick to the *Three Words* and you will most likely welcome changes from internet search engines. You will see the many benefits your adherence to these *Three Words* provides in terms of your rankings on search engines as well as positive behavior from potential customers.

Before we look at the basic fundamentals of SEO for each type of search, let's first review how to identify the keywords associated with your business. Knowing how to identify and keep up to date on keywords and keyword phrases that are relevant to your business are essential to SEO for all types of searches and will be extremely useful to all your internet marketing strategies and the ingredients you assemble to formulate a winning recipe.

In the previous chapter (Ingredient 1), we covered the Google Keyword Tool (googlekeywordtool.com). This is a great place to start identifying the keywords associated with your business. Simply type in a single word or a group of words (phrase) and the Google Keyword Tool will provide you with information about how many searches your keyword or keyword phrase receives on a monthly basis as well as a long list of keyword ideas that have a close relationship to your keyword as well as the monthly search activity for those keyword ideas.

Another great way to identify keywords and keyword phrases is to conduct test searches on the popular search engines of Google, Yahoo and Bing. For example, go to Google (google.com) and perform a search on the keyword phrase "green beans". Google will list or rank a variety of search results for the keyword phrase "green beans". Google will also provide you with a section (usually found at the bottom of the page) titled: *Searches related to green beans.* The following is a sample of what that looks like:

Searches related to **green beans**

growing green beans	fresh green beans
green beans **recipe**	steamed green beans
green beans **nutrition**	green beans **calories**
how to cook green beans	green beans **coffee**

1 2 3 4 5 6 7 8 9 10   Next

Note how Google automatically provides you with keyword phrases that are closely related to your keyword or keyword phrase.

Just like Google, Yahoo and Bing will provide you with keywords and keyword phrases related to your search. Here's a list of related keyword phrases for the "green beans" search on Yahoo:

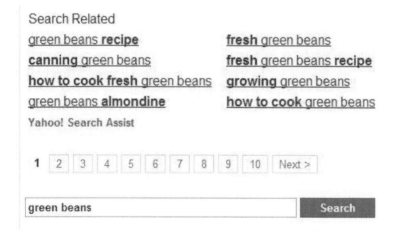

Here's a list for the "green beans" search on Bing:

Related searches for **green beans**

Types of Green Beans	Green Beans Growing
Planting Green Beans	Green Bean Recipes
Cooking Green Beans	Green Beans Nutrition
Nutritional Value of Green Beans	Canned Green Bean Recipes

1   2   3   4   5   Next

Using the keyword tools that can be found on the internet as well as the information provided by search engines related to your keyword testing, you will be able to assemble a high quality and highly relevant core group of keywords to utilize in all your SEO strategies and efforts.

Analytics tools are also important in identifying and refining keywords. These reports and the information contained within them will provide you information about the actual keywords and keyword phrases that visitors to your website used to find you. You can take this keyword information and apply it to your SEO. In addition, this same information can be utilized as a source for developing new keywords and keyword phrases that are closely related.

Two popular analytics tools for keywords and keyword phrases that are handy are Google Analytics and Google Webmaster Tools. We will go into more detail about these analytics tools in a later chapter of this book.

Now let's look at the SEO fundamentals for each type of internet search. Referencing the list below, note the different types of searches that can be conducted on Google.

You will see the following options:

1. Web
2. Images
3. Maps
4. Shopping
5. News
6. More

The "More" option currently provides a submenu for conducting specific searches for the following:

1. Videos
2. Books
3. Blogs
4. Flights
5. Discussions
6. Recipes
7. Applications
8. Patents

(See below example from Google)

As you can see, there are many opportunities to gain visibility on the internet, and you should evaluate whether each option is right for your business. Whatever opportunities you choose to pursue, you need to understand search engine optimization for each and implement strategies, plans and tactics that will maximize your visibility and increase visits to your website.

General Web Search

The general searches conducted on the web will provide all types of search results. For the keyword phrase of "green beans", a search on any of the popular search engines will provide you with websites about green beans, photos about green beans, recipes for green beans, news articles about green beans, blog articles about green beans and more.

Your website should be optimized so you can be easily found and indexed by search engines and thereby seen by people conducting searches on these search engines. How do you do this? The structure of your website and what's contained in your website play big roles –as do the majority of the "Ingredients" and topics found throughout this book.

Here's a checklist for your website:

Website Written Content

 The written content on your website should be **original and authentic (don't duplicate written content from other websites)** and contain keywords and keyword phrases that are relevant based on the keyword research conducted. Don't get too carried away with using keywords and keyword phrases in the written copy of your website. Many websites over-use keywords and keyword phrases. If your website content is simple to read and conversational style, it will receive positive response from both the people visiting your website and from the search engines.

Website Page Titles

Each page of your website should have page titles that contain keywords that are relevant to your business and unique to the written content of that page. Most search engines only use a maximum of 60-70 characters in a page title. Therefore, anything over 60-70 will typically not be picked up.

Website Page Descriptions

Each page of your website should have a unique description of what that page is about and incorporate relevant keywords. Most search engines only use 160 characters in a page description. Therefore, you should limit your description to a maximum of 160 characters.

Website Page Keywords

For each page of your website, list the keyword or keywords that are relevant and specific to that page.

Website Images

Use images on each page of your website. Each of the images should be given a file name that contains keywords related to the picture. Each picture should also be given a brief "ALT" tag description that is unique and relevant for that picture. More information about the images you use on the internet is covered below in the section titled "Image Search".

Website Videos

Videos are an effective tool to enhance the visitor experience on your website as we will cover in more detail in a later chapter. They are also an excellent way to attract search engines. Videos uploaded and embedded on your website should be tagged with the keywords that are relevant to the video and your business. Also include written transcripts for each of your videos to maximize the effectiveness of each video. More information about the videos you use on the internet is covered below in the section titled "Video Search".

Website Blog

A blog and the blog articles produced for your website's blog are very important features of your website and another "Ingredient" of success as will be discussed in a later chapter. Each blog article should be optimized for the search engines using unique and relevant titles, written content, keywords, descriptions, images and links.

Website Site Maps

Sitemaps provide websites with a higher level of organization that search engines such as Google like to see. A Sitemap is basically a list of the pages and content contained within your website all located in one file that makes it convenient for the search engines to understand your website and how to crawl it. You can think of a Sitemap as being similar to an outline for a research paper or the table of contents for a book.

Many times, a sitemap is something that can be made accessible to search engines on the back end of your website design. Webmasters generally follow this method. A public accessible sitemap is generally not needed for a well laid out website.

Website Links

The use of links within your website is very important for both internal links (links to content found within your website) and external links (links to content found outside of your website on the internet). When using links, the relevancy of what you are linking to is much more important than the quantity of links you create.

Some people utilize something called a "link exchange" to generate links to their website. This is a process where website owners can "exchange" or post a link for each other on their respective websites. However, be sure that other site is relevant to your own site - as well as an authentic. Exchanging links with "spammy" websites will hurt your site more than help it.

Image Search

The way you use and handle images (photos) on the internet can be extremely beneficial to your overall on-line visibility. Like all content, search engines want to provide their users with the best quality and most relevant images for any given search being conducted.

Here's a checklist for the images you use on your website and the internet:

Image Quality: Make sure the images you use on your website and throughout the internet are clear, sharp and easy to see. Blurry or unclear photos are hard for people to see and do not provide a good user experience. In addition, poor quality photos do not reflect well on your business and the professional image it is trying to cultivate with potential customers.

File Name: Use unique file names for images that describe the image. Incorporating a relevant keyword in the image file name is also a beneficial practice.

Here are examples of poorly named image files:

Img0001.jpg

Stock0022.jpg

Photo12.jpg

Here are examples of image files that have been properly named:

Kentucky-blue-green-beans.jpg

Green-bean-casserole.jpg

Green-bean-sprout.jpg

Note how these image file names are specific. You should also take into consideration the location of the photo when giving it an image file name. For example, if you created a page on your website that targets "How to grow green beans in a jar", you should place a photo on that website page of a green bean plant growing in a jar to augment the written content on the page. The image file name for the photo should be something along the lines of *growing-green-beans-in-a-jar.jpg.*

Alt Text: The "alt" attribute of an image being used on the internet is a way for you to describe the photo. Using the above example for growing green beans in a jar, the Alt Text used for the photo should be something like: **growing green beans in a jar**.

Original and Authentic Photography: There is a very large supply of stock photography that is easy to access and utilize. However, original photography should be used whenever possible. Hiring a professional photographer and/or purchasing a camera that takes high quality digital photos will be worth the investment. These original and authentic photos can be used in all types of marketing and advertising for your business.

Map Search

When people use the "Map Search" option on search engines, they are most likely trying to find the location of something on a map along with directions for getting there. If your business has one office or many offices, you want to be easy to find via Map Searches so people can find you.

To get found in Map Searches, list your business location on your website. If you have more than one location, list each of the individual locations and create a separate page on your website for each of the office/store locations.

You will also want to create local business accounts on the major search engines of Google, Yahoo and Bing. If your business has more than one location, each of the accounts will allow you to create a listing for all locations.

Local business accounts will be covered in more detail in a later chapter. They are important for a variety of reasons, not just map searches.

Shopping Search

If you have a product you sell either on-line or in your store location(s), the Shopping Search option on search engines is probably somewhere you want your products to show up.

Getting your product to show up in the Shopping Search option for search engines typically requires the establishment of a merchant account with the respective search engine. For example, to get your product listed on Google Shopping, you first need to set-up an account with Google Merchant Center. From there, Google provides you with instructions for submitting your products.

News Search

The News Search option on search engines provides users with a convenient way for searching the latest news on any topic that interests them. As you might expect, the search results for a topic using this method are pulled from a variety of news sources.

When it comes to maximizing the visibility of your business, press releases are an effective tool to gain visibility in News Search. Press releases are one of the "Ingredients" for success covered in this book and will be discussed in more detail in a later chapter.

A strategy of routinely submitting original on-line press releases relating to your business can drive a significant amount of traffic to your website.

Video Search

Videos are a very popular feature for website users. As a result, people using search engines frequently conduct video searches. Having your videos show up in these internet searches provides excellent opportunities to drive traffic to your website and/or new business.

Here's a checklist for the videos you use on your website and the internet:

Video Quality: Make sure the videos provide a good user experience. That means you can both clearly see and hear the video.

Original Video: Just like stock photography, there is a huge supply of stock video footage that can be obtained. However, original video footage produced specifically for your business will provide the best results in the long run.

Video File Name: Use unique and descriptive file names for your video files. Incorporating a relevant keyword in the image file name is also beneficial.

Here are examples of poorly named image files:

Video0001.mp4

Stockvideo0001.mov

01022013.mp4

Here are examples of video files that have been properly named:

Growing-green-beans.mp4

How-to-make -green-bean-casserole.mov

Just like with the naming of image files, note how these video file names are specific. You should also take into consideration the location of the video when giving it a video file name. For example, if you created a page on your website that targets "How to grow green beans in a jar", you should place a video on that website page about growing green beans in a jar to augment the content on the page. The video file name for the photo should be something along the lines of *growing-green-beans-in-a-jar.mp4.*

Video Title: The title of each video should be unique and incorporate a relevant keyword or keyword phrase.

Video Description: Write unique video descriptions that are accurate about what the video is about and incorporate relevant keywords.

Video Tags: Videos can be "tagged" with keywords. Include tags that are relevant to what the video is about.

More information about videos and their use as an "Ingredient" for success will be provided in a later chapter of this book.

Understanding the basics of search engine optimization and the different ways to be found by internet search engines are an essential "Ingredient" in the recipe for successfully marketing your business. Make sure you are taking the necessary steps to maximize your SEO efforts and stay up to date on the latest changes being made by search engines so you can react accordingly.

Ingredient **3**

Update Your Website Monthly

Fishing has two main strategies. Under strategy number 1, you bait your hook, throw your line in the water and just leave it out there until a fish comes along and decides they are hungry enough to take the bait. Under strategy number 2, you bait your hook, throw your line in the water and wait a little bit. Then, if nothing happens, you reel in your line and check your bait. Sometimes the bait will not be there. A fish may have eaten the bait without the hook going into the fish's mouth, the bait may have fallen off the hook or the bait may have died (if you are using live bait).

After more than 40 years of fishing, we have found that strategy number 2 catches way more fish than strategy number 1. Letting your line sit in the water without ever checking it and making changes doesn't catch very many fish.

Building and launching a website takes a lot of time and effort. If you have gone through this process, you will appreciate exactly what that statement really means. Unfortunately, a lot of people think when their website is launched, their work is done. It's time to hit cruise control and coast for awhile. That's a big mistake.

Once your website is up and running, it should be updated each and every month. Search engines like websites that have fresh content. Most of all, people who are searching for your product or service like to see websites that are fresh too.

So what should you be updating? Almost everything, including:

1. Updates to existing pages of the website.
2. Add new pages.
3. Add new videos.
4. Add new photos.
5. Add new blog articles.
6. Add new outbound links to relevant and authoritative sites.

(Be aware of not having too many outbound links, especially without reciprocal inbound links.)

It doesn't have to be all of the above in one month, but it should be two or three of the above. This is not a task that requires a significant amount of time, but it is very important. If your direct competition is doing it, you must do it. If your competition isn't, then you have a huge opportunity to get ahead.

Routinely updating your website on a monthly basis will improve your organic rankings on search engines. It will also improve your chances of turning those who visit your website into new business.

The quality effort and time invested in your website will yield positive results. Failure to invest time and effort will have the opposite effect.

When you do make changes to your website, make sure to track what you have done. Start a log and write down all the changes you make. Over time, compare these changes to your website's analytics data. You will begin to see how your changes improve performance.

Ingredient 4

In-Bound Links, Out-Bound Links

Remember the research papers you had to write in high school and college?

In the days before the internet became the powerful tool it is today, students went to a library to collect information for their research papers.

If you are over the age of 35, you probably logged countless hours at a library flipping through card catalogues and wandering the aisles scanning where the Dewey Decimal System placed the books you needed. You went to the library because that's where the information was located.

You found thousands and thousands of books, magazines, newspapers, pamphlets and film produced and written from authors from all over the world. You used that information to support statements, theories and conclusions you wrote about in your research papers. To properly write a research paper, you included footnotes and a reference section at the end of the paper.

If that library was a website, all the various footnotes and references that were included in all the research papers written by every student who used that library for sources of information would be considered in-bounds links. You want your website to become that library.

In-bound links tell search engines the information found on your website is important. You're the library that everyone goes to. In-bound links help your website build the powerful mix of relevance and authority that's needed to rank high on internet search engines.

Quality is More Important than Quantity

There was a time when the volume of in-bound links to a website was very important to rank high on search engines. Over the years, webmasters (people who oversee the performance of a website) used tactics to generate as many in-bound links to the website as possible regardless as to whether those in-bound links came from credible sources or not. That's not the case anymore. Now, the mere volume of in-bound links to a website is not as important as the over-all quality of the in-bound links.

Using the green bean example from a previous chapter, let's pretend you own a farm in Ohio that produces nothing but green beans. You have a website for your farm that contains all types of wonderful information about green beans. You list the different kinds of green beans. You list the history of how the green bean was developed. You include different ways to grow greens beans. You feature a variety of popular green bean recipes. If someone wants to know something about green beans, your website probably has something about it.

The city in Ohio near your green bean farm has a fabulous whole foods market that's full of different products from around the region. The owners of the whole foods market have an on-line blog where they routinely post a variety of articles about their market and the products offered. This blog has become very popular with residents of the area. There are over 100,000 people that subscribe to the blog and read the articles that are published. One of the blog articles the owners of the whole foods market has written is about green beans. Within that blog article they link to your website. That's a high quality in-bound link for you. You want as many of these high quality in-bound links as possible.

In a comparison example, let's turn the tables. A furniture manufacturer located in China has a blog and writes an article about sofas. Within that blog article, they link to your website (a green bean farm located in Ohio). This is not a high quality link. It's not relevant to your business or your product. It's not relevant to your location. It's not relevant to anything you talk about on your website. It's a poor quality link. Too many of these links will hurt your website and its ability to rank high on search engines.

How Do You Get High Quality In-Bound Links?

Generating high quality in-bound links takes a multi-faceted approach.

First and foremost is the need to produce content on your website that is original, meaningful and interesting. That includes written content, videos, photography and blog articles. Over time, the quality of your content will get noticed if you promote and advertise it properly. When it does get noticed, other users of the very powerful tool we call the internet will link to your website and create in-bound links.

Reach out to others and request link exchanges. Using the green bean farm example from above, it would be beneficial for you to ask the owners of the whole foods market to exchange links to each others' websites. It would also be beneficial to ask the whole foods market owners if you could occasionally provide them with guest articles for their blog and vice versa.

Establishing local business accounts on internet search engines and creating citations on internet directory websites all offer you opportunities to create in-bound links to your website. We will cover search engine local business accounts and internet directory websites in the chapters that follow.

Write press releases about your business and publish them on a variety of press release websites and newspaper websites. When you publish press releases on-line, you will usually have an opportunity to link to your website. We will cover press releases in an upcoming chapter.

Produce videos and publish the videos on the many video internet sites like YouTube. When you upload a video to YouTube, you have an opportunity to insert a link to your website in the video's description. This is another area we will address in a later chapter.

Take great photos and share the photos on-line. When someone uses one of your photos, make sure you require them to add a link back to your website in the photo.

Constantly be on the look-out for opportunities to generate in-bound links. The internet is an ever-changing environment. New tools for creating quality in-bound links are certain to be on the horizon. Remember, quality is what matters most.

Outbound Links

It's also beneficial for you to be generating high-quality out-bound links. When writing new pages and blog articles, be sure to include at least one outbound link to a credible and relevant website.

Once again using your green bean farm website as an example, let's assume you are adding a new page to your website that talks about the nutritional value of green beans. It would be beneficial to insert an out-bound link on this new page of your website to a credible web site that supports your statements about the nutritional benefits of green beans. An excellent choice for the outbound link would be the U.S. Department of Agriculture website's page relating to green beans.

Both in-bound links and out-bound links are very important ingredients for success. Remember to avoid linking tactics that try to play games with the search engines. That will harm your website in the long run. Creating high-quality in-bound and out-bound links that are relevant to your business is the strategy that works.

Ingredient **5**

Local Business Accounts on Search Engines

Currently the three most popular search engines on the internet are Google, Bing and Yahoo. We like to call them the "Big 3". Google is by far the biggest with an estimated 900 million monthly visitors. Bing is a distant second with an estimated 165 million monthly visitors. Yahoo is close behind with an estimated 160 million monthly visitors. Add up the monthly visitors to the Big 3 and the total is over 1.2 billion. That's nearly 15% of the entire world's population!

If you want your business to be found on the internet, you must pay attention to what the Big 3 search engines are doing and what features they offer. One of these features is a local business account. You should have a local business account on Google first. Then, you should establish a local business account on both Bing and Yahoo.

Local SEO or Local Search Engine Optimization has rapidly gained importance. The major search engines want to provide their users with high quality, accurate and relevant information. Local business accounts are a way for the search engines to do just that. Those businesses that spend the time creating and maintaining a local business account on each of the Big 3 will be rewarded with increased on-line visibility.

To set-up local business accounts on each of the Big 3, visit these URL's:

Google Places for Business (Now Google + Local)
https://www.google.com/business/placesforbusiness/

BING Places for Business
https://www.bingplaces.com/

Yahoo Small Business Local Listings
http://smallbusiness.yahoo.com/local-listings/

When you visit each of the above links to each of the Big 3 search engine's local business accounts, easy-to-follow instructions to set-up your account are provided. Here are some tips when creating your local business listings:

1. Be prepared to spend some time establishing the listings. You will be asked to verify who you are and your authorization to add or edit the account either by email or telephone.

2. Make sure your business telephone number is correct.

3. If you list another telephone number on your website (for example, a toll-free telephone number), be sure to include that on your local business listing. The listing will allow you to input more than one telephone number.

4. Make sure the link you include on your account is "deep-linking" into your website. Don't just link to the Home Page of your website. If your business is located in Cleveland, Ohio, then create a specific page for your website with your Cleveland location and link your local business account to that location page.

5. Make sure you fill out all fields of the local business account listing. Listings that are 100% complete are important. That includes uploading photos and videos if you have them.

6. Make sure your name, address and telephone information is accurate <u>and</u> consistent with what is listed on your website. For example, if your business is:

> Green Bean Farms, LLC
> 1234 Main Street
> Cleveland, OH 44444
> (555) 555-5555

Make sure that is <u>exactly</u> the way it is listed on all your local business accounts. The consistency of your information is very important. The local SEO term for this is called NAP. It stands for Name, Address and Phone number. NAP is critical for businesses who want to rank well on the search engines.

7. When you have entered all the information to set-up your account, you will be asked to verify the account before it is activated. This verification process will be either a telephone call to your business telephone number you provided on your listing or a postcard in the mail to your business address. In both cases, you will be provided with a verification code that must be entered in order for your listing to go live. Postcards can take between 7-10 days to arrive via the U.S. Mail. This verification process is one of the primary tools the search engines use to make sure your business is valid. Once you go through this validation process, it provides the search engines with the assurances they are looking for in order to properly rank your business.

When your local business account is active, don't forget about it. Make sure you are monitoring it, ensuring your business profile is always up to date and accurate. Additionally and once your local business account has been active for awhile, there will be valuable analytical information provided by your local business account that you can use throughout your marketing and advertising.

You will be able to see how many times your local business listing appeared on the search engines. These are known as Impressions. The more Impressions your listing receives, the higher the probability someone will see it and take action.

You will also see what keyword search terms are generating Impressions for your local business listing. This is helpful to maximize all your SEO efforts.

Another valuable piece of information provided by your local business listing is the actions people take when they view your listing. You will see if they clicked through to your website. You will also see if they clicked for driving directions to your business and where those driving direction requests came from. This is very useful in determining what geographical areas people interested in your business are coming from. The information can be used to target these geographical regions using other "ingredients" contained within this book.

Local business accounts on the Big 3 search engines also allow people to post reviews about your business. When it comes to marketing, there is nothing better than a testimonial from a satisfied customer. Posting a review on your local business account is something you want to encourage your customers to do.

Reviews are also one of the reasons you want to continually monitor your local business accounts. People can post favorable reviews but they also can post unfavorable reviews. You need to check to see the types of reviews people are posting. This can be very beneficial to help you identify problems that need addressed or strengths that should be exploited.

Ingredient **6**

Citations
(Internet Directory Business Listings)

How many quality on-line citations does your business have?

It's a question not many business owners can quickly answer. But if they want to get ranked high on internet search engines they should be able to do this.

When other websites list your business, it's called a citation. Why are citations important? If you go back to the beginning of this book in the section titled: *Three (3) Important Words to Remember Before We Begin,* you learned the importance of

(1) Relevance (2) Authenticity and (3) Authority. Citations play a very important part in establishing and enhancing the on-line Relevance, Authenticity and Authority for your business and your website. Implementing and maintaining a citation building strategy is another important Ingredient for successfully marketing your business.

When it comes to building your internet citations, consistently growing a quality list of citations is more important than the overall quantity of your citations. Note how throughout this book we emphasize the importance of "quality" vs. "quantity". It's a strategy that will serve you well in the long run.

So how do you identify quality internet sites to list your business and continually build quality citations? We will give you some high quality sites to get you going and tools for generating citations ideas.

Here's a list of 20 high-quality internet sites to get your business citation building efforts moving in the right direction:

1. Google Places for Business
2. BING Places for Business
3. Yahoo Small Business Listings
(The above should sound familiar. We gave them special attention in the previous chapter.)
4. Facebook
5. Twitter
6. Linked-In
7. Merchant Circle
8. Manta
9. MapQuest
10. Hotfrog

11. YP.com
12. Local.com
13. Yelp
14. Localeze
15. BBB.org (Better Business Bureau)
16. Foursquare.com
17. Superpages.com
18. ChamberofCommerce.com
19. Whitepages.com
20. Citysearch.com

We will cover some additional citation sources in future Ingredients. Just remember, there are many, many more opportunities to build citations on the internet. In fact, the number of potential sites in which to build your citations is constantly changing. Sites get deleted and added all the time. A good strategy and practice is to routinely identify and add new citations for your business monthly.

There are several good tools readily available on the internet to help with citations. One we like to use is BrightLocal (brightlocal.com). When you set-up an account on BrightLocal, one of the features they have is called "Citation Tracker". It identifies citations your business has obtained. It also lists potential new citation opportunities along with an assigned "citation value" to each listing so you can pick the sites that will be the most beneficial to your business and your website. Here's an example:

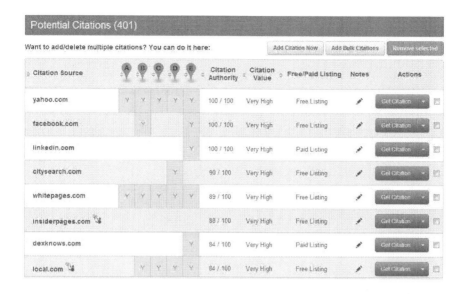

Note the columns of the report labeled "Citation Authority" and "Citation Value". This is how you can identify quality sites that will be of benefit to your business and your website.

When you create listings on the various internet directory sites, it's very important not to have duplicate listings. If you accidentally create a duplicate listing or discover there is a duplicate listing on a particular directory site, delete the duplicate.

It's also very important to make sure your business name, address and telephone number (NAP) match exactly with what's on your website. As outlined in the previous chapter, it's critical that your NAP remain consistent throughout the internet.

Correctly building citations on the internet is a time consuming process. It's important to maximize each of your listings on each directory site. That means filling out all the fields, uploading photos and going through a verifications process. Utilize what each listing has to offer and don't forget to link your listing to your website! This creates a quality in-bound link. When you do link your citation to your website, try to make it a deep link to an internal page of your website vs. linking to the Home Page of your website. For example, if your website has a Location Page (and it should), link your citation to that page instead of your Home Page.

All the time you spend on building citations will be rewarded with higher visibility on the internet, more visitors to your website and more leads to convert into sales.

This is an Ingredient most businesses don't take full advantage of and one that can set you apart from your competition. Remember when creating citations, focus on the quality of your citations. It's important to have citations that are complete as compared to a bunch of citations that are incomplete.

The quantity of citations your business has does make a difference, but so does the quality of those citations.

Ingredient 7

Blog

In a previous chapter, we talked about Ingredient 3 in our Mix of Ingredients - *Update Your Website Monthly*. A blog is a great way to do this. In fact, a blog is an essential marketing tool for many reasons.

To be successful on the internet, you need to generate original and authentic content. As outlined in a previous chapter, content includes written words, photography and video. A blog is used to deliver one of these pieces of content or a variety of content. A blog is versatile.

Your blog is also a method to build highly relevant links. Every blog article you write and publish on your website should contain one or more of the following types of links:

- A link to a relevant page within your website. (internal link)
- A link to a previously written blog article. (internal link)
- A link to a relevant, authentic and authoritative external website that supports the topic of your blog or provides additional information. (outbound link)

Each blog article should focus on a certain topic and a specific keyword, known as a focus keyword. Include the focus keyword in:

- The Article Title / Heading of your blog article.
- The URL of your blog article.
- The meta description of your blog article.
- The photo Alt Tag you include within your blog article.
- The Page Title of your blog.
- The content of your blog. (However, don't overuse the focus keyword.)

The majority of your blog articles should revolve around the topics associated with your business. However, it's also important to mix it up and write about other topics. These can include local events, local issues and other topics that people find interesting. To make your blogging easy, planning is essential. Determine what topics your blog posts will be about at the beginning of each month. Get employees to suggest ideas. You can even get your customers to suggest ideas by asking them in person, surveying them on your website, surveying them with an email marketing campaign or posting questions for comments on social media.

There is no magic formula for determining how frequently you should post an article on your website's blog. At a minimum you should post at least one or two articles per month. If you're business is in a highly competitive industry or market, it should be multiple times per month. Sometimes, it's necessary to post a blog article several times each week. No matter which formula you follow, you should be consistent.

Each of your blog articles should contain at least 250 words, but it should not be too lengthy. Blog articles are intended to be read quickly. It's also a good idea to insert photography into each blog article. Photography is beneficial to both SEO as well as engaging readers. Like the old saying goes, "A picture is worth a thousand words". Whenever possible, make the photos you insert into your blog articles original photography instead of stock photography.

Over time, a blog that is properly implemented and maintained will usually generate a growing list of followers. That's when your blog will jump to another level. Encourage followers to post comments and questions on your blog. Make sure to monitor those comments and respond to questions promptly. A blog that engages readers will often be shared by those readers with their network of contacts. Beneficial blog articles on interesting topics will also get referenced by other bloggers. This generates inbound links to your website. That's powerful!

When blogging, always remember to keep your personal opinions on controversial subjects to yourself. You never know how your opinions will be received. The purpose of your blog is to generate new business. Don't take the chance of alienating business relationships you are trying to foster. It's a good rule of thumb not to make blog posts about religion, politics and moral beliefs – unless that is the nature of your blog or business. If you're a political blogger, you will obviously be writing about politics.

Finally, always be authentic and original with your blog articles. Never duplicate content from others or yourself.

A blog on your website will keep your website fresh and updated. It will also create "Authority" which is one of the **_Three Important Words to Remember_**. The time and effort you invest in your blog will be rewarded by the search engines with favorable organic rankings.

A blog is a very important Ingredient in your recipe for success!

Ingredient **8**

Press Releases (On-line and Off-line)

Throughout this book, there is a primary focus on taking advantage of on-line opportunities. All these internet-related Ingredients are very important to your overall marketing success. However, traditional forms of marketing cannot and should not be ignored. These forms of marketing are equally important Ingredients. Just like any food recipe, when you start to omit ingredients, the recipe isn't as good and doesn't taste like it should.

Press releases are great examples that support the above statement. This traditional form of marketing and public relations remains a worthwhile tool today. In fact, the internet has provided more opportunities to enhance how a press release gets utilized.

First let's talk about what topics are worthy of issuing a press release for your business. There are opportunities that present themselves continually when you are focused on press releases. The following are some example ideas, though this is by no means an all-inclusive list:

- New employee joins your company.
- You or an employee is a speaker at an event.
- Your business sponsors a charity, little league team, event, etc.
- Your business launches a new product or service.
- One of your customers or patients is doing something extraordinary like climbing a mountain, running the Boston Marathon or dedicating their time to helping people with special needs.
- You join a local association or group.

The list could go on and on. The thing to remember is to come up with press release ideas that are authentic, relevant and genuine. Press releases should not be directly trying to "sell" nor should they be "gimmicky". If they are, they probably won't get picked up either on-line or off-line, providing you with no real benefit.

When you write a press release, there is a specific format to follow. This includes:

- Title
- Subtitle
- Body
- Quotes from people who are associated with the story

- A section specifically about your business with your telephone number and website
- Media contact information

Here's an example of a press release format:

FOR IMMEDIATE RELEASE
January 1, 2013

XYZ AUTO PARTS WELCOMES JOHN SMITH AS NEW GENERAL MANAGER

XYZ Auto Parts with four store locations in the greater Toledo area announced today that John Doe has joined the company as its new general manager.

A native of Toledo, Mr. Doe attended Woodward High School and the University of Toledo, graduating with a degree in business. He is an active member of the Toledo Area Chamber of Commerce and a sits on the board for Toledo Inner-City Little League.

"We are extremely excited to have John join our company", stated Bill Smith, owner of XYZ Auto Parts. "He brings a wealth of experience to our auto parts stores having first been an auto mechanic, then spending the last 20 years working his way up through the auto parts industry. His knowledge of automobiles and parts is amazing", he added.

"I am honored to be a part of XYZ Auto Parts", exclaimed John Doe. "This is a wonderful organization focused on customer service and providing the best quality parts at the lowest prices."

Mr. Doe will be based at the company's Airport Highway store location.

About XYZ Auto Parts

XYZ Auto Parts is the Toledo, Ohio area leader in providing quality auto parts at the lowest prices. Founded in 1958 by renowned local mechanic Joe Smith, this Toledo based business has four auto parts stores located on 1234 Airport Highway, 5678 Sylvania Avenue, 9876 Anthony Wayne Trail and 5432 Detroit Ave. Store hours at each location are from 6:00am – 8:00pm Monday through Saturday. For additional information, please call (555) 555-5555 or visit the website at XYZAutoParts.com.

Media Contact:
Ms. Sue Smith
Marketing Director
Telephone: (555) 555-5555
Email: **sue.smith@xyzauto.com**

Once you have written your press release, it should be submitted for both on-line and off-line use. Though there are countless outlets to submit your release to, the information that follows should get you started.

First, research your local newspapers -both the big newspapers and the smaller local neighborhood newspapers. Most of these newspapers have a website with a feature that allows you to submit your news to that newspaper.

For example, the website for the Akron Beacon Journal newspaper in Akron, Ohio is www.ohio.com. On this site is a feature called "UPublish". When you select this feature, it allows you to submit your press release. The submission is reviewed by the newspaper's staff and if proper, published on the newspaper's website. It may also be published in the print edition of the newspaper.

Similar features like the "UPublish" tool can be found on most newspaper websites throughout the United States. If the newspaper does not have a news submission tool, visit the Contact Page of the newspaper's website. They typically list the names, telephone numbers and email addresses of the staff including reporters and editors. Then, email your press release to the applicable staff member or pick up the telephone and call them to ask if they would be interested in receiving your press release.

Developing relationships with your local newspaper or newspapers is a beneficial long term strategy for you and your business. Write a personal letter to a staff reporter at your local newspaper telling them about yourself and your business. Invite them to contact you for quotes when they are writing a story that is related to your industry. Give them your personal email address and personal cell phone number. When they do call, make sure you are available to take the call – make the time! They are writing with strict deadlines and most likely do not have time to wait for your return phone call. You don't want to miss the opportunity to get yourself or your business mentioned in their stories.

Don't forget about other local publications. Newsletters and magazines are also looking for interesting local news stories for their publications. Research their websites and contact information just like the newspapers. Also work to develop relationships with staff members at these publications for a mutually beneficial relationship.

There are many opportunities to publish your press releases on-line. Some of these services are free and others are paid. With these types of on-line press releases you will usually get what you pay for. If you use the free services, you won't get much in terms of exposure or search engine optimization (SEO) benefits. The paid services will provide you with the opportunities to maximize your visibility and generate links to your website which are beneficial for SEO.

There are many on-line press release services to take advantage of with pricing from around $20 per press release to several hundred dollars per release. There are also options for monthly subscriptions where you can submit a specific number of press releases for the monthly subscription fee amount. These are usually much more cost effective than the pay per press release option. Here are a few suggestions for publishing your press release on-line:

- PRWeb.com
- SBWire.com
- FreePressRelease.com

When you utilize the on-line press release services, your press release will be distributed to a network of news wires like Associated Press, Google News and Yahoo News. If one of these news wires likes what they see, they pick-up your press release and publish it. That will mostly likely be one of the best marketing investment you will probably have made.

Press releases are an essential Ingredient to your marketing success. Take full advantage of what they can do for your business.

Ingredient **9**

Pay Per Click

Pay Per Click or PPC is an important Ingredient that allows you to get immediate visibility on certain internet search engines and social media sites. When you run a Pay Per Click Campaign, you will be charged each time someone "clicks" on your pay Pay Per Click Advertisement. When a person does "click" on your advertisement, it takes them to your website. The placement of your PPC advertisement is based on an amount you bid for that placement. Here's an example of PPC advertisements on the Google search engine when someone is conducting a search using the keyword phrase "auto parts".

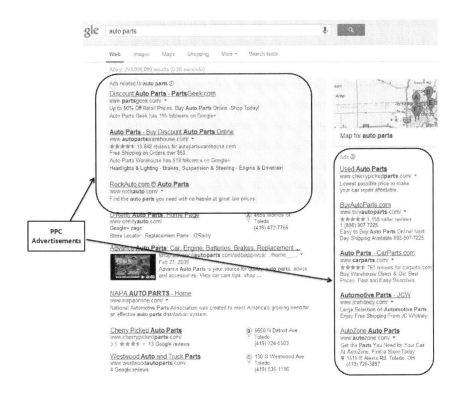

Note the strategic placement and positions of the PPC advertisements at the top of the page and a separate and distinct right-hand column. These are both highly visible areas and they capture attention. In order for your PPC advertisement to be at the top of the page, you bid for that position. If you bid high enough, your advertisement will be placed at the top. The amount of the bid needed to secure this top position is determined by the amount of competition for the keyword phrase being used. For some keywords, the bid amount is less than $1 per click. For other highly popular keywords with a lot of competition, the bid could be $30 per click or even much more.

We could write a separate book entirely about pay per click. There are a lot of details and moving parts associated with pay per click campaigns. The purpose of this chapter is to make you aware of different PPC opportunities and why they are an important Ingredient in a winning marketing strategy.

First, let's look at why PPC is an Ingredient. Advertising is about getting your message in front of people. Everyone understands that. When it comes to being found on internet search engines like Google, BING and Yahoo, it comes down to organic search results and pay per click. To get highly visible organic rankings on search engines, it takes time. With PPC, you can obtain visibility literally the same day. Both organic search rankings and PPC are Ingredients we recommend so that you maximize your visibility on search engines.

PPC campaigns are easily controlled, managed and tracked.

- You can budget the amount of money you want to spend on PPC.
- You can select specific and targeted keywords to display your PPC advertisement.
- You can limit where the advertisements are shown to a defined geographical region.
- You can control the date of when the PPC campaign will start and the date of when it will end. This can be especially useful for date sensitive campaigns like contents and special offers.

- You can see how many times your advertisements are being displayed (known as "Impressions").
- You can see the number of times your advertisement is being "clicked".
- You also have the ability to see if that "click" to your website resulted in a telephone call or message to your

business (the term for this is "Conversion"). You can also take it a step further and see if the telephone call or message to your business created a sale and how much that sale was worth.

- When you do all of this, you will be able to determine your "Return on Investment" or "ROI".

Consider the following example of how that is useful using our fictitious XYZ Auto Parts company from a previous chapter:

John Doe is the general manager for XYZ Auto Parts. He would like to increase sales for windshield wiper blades at all his stores in the Toledo, Ohio area. John got with his team, and they developed a plan to market and advertise a windshield wiper blade promotion. One of the tools they will be using is PPC.

They set up a PPC campaign on Google Adwords to start on October 1st and end on November 30th. They budgeted an amount of $50 per day to spend on the PPC campaign. They limited the campaign to only show up for people searching on Google who lived within 10 miles of each of their auto parts stores. They wrote their PPC advertisement and linked it to a special page on their website that was created just for this windshield wiper blade promotion where people could download a coupon.

Two weeks into the campaign on October 15th, John asked to see the numbers on the PPC campaign for the windshield wiper blade promotion. Here's the information he was provided:

Windshield Wiper Blade PPC Campaign

Impressions - 23,879
Clicks - 358
Total Cost - $750
Average Cost Per Click - $2.09
Conversions – 107
Cost Per Conversion - $7.01
Sales – 81
Total Sales Revenue - $2,592
ROI – 29%

Based on the above information, John decided to continue the PPC campaign because the ROI was in a range of where he wanted it to be.

John continued to check the PPC campaign every two weeks, making adjustments along the way to optimize performance.

The above example shows how a PPC campaign can be effective. PPC provides high visibility with a lot of control.

The one thing to remember with any PPC campaign is to constantly monitor it so you can control it. If you put your PPC campaigns on auto-pilot and don't monitor them, you can spend a lot of money with little to show for it. Information is power and PPC provides a lot of good information.

So where are the opportunities to run PPC campaigns? There are many. We will highlight the PPC opportunities that have been productive in our experience:

Google Adwords – adwords.google.com

This is Google's option to run PPC campaigns. Given all the activity the Google search engine produces. This is where you will want to start. If you have videos that you have produced for your business, you can run video PPC campaigns on YouTube using Google Adwords.

BING Ads – bingads.microsoft.com

BING and Yahoo combined forces for PPC. When you establish an account on BING Ads, you are gaining access to both BING and Yahoo for your PPC campaigns.

Facebook

Facebook provides options for PPC campaigns and to promote the posts you make on your Facebook business page. When running Facebook PPC campaigns and promoted posts, your strategy is different than running campaigns on Google, BING and Yahoo. We will review Facebook strategies in more detail in a later chapter.

Linked-In

Linked-In is a popular social networking tool for business professionals. If you are in a business where you want to target these professionals, Linked-In is a good way to reach them. Similar to Facebook, your Linked-In PPC strategy and advertising messages are going to be unique for Linked-In.

As stated earlier, there are many details with PPC campaigns that are not being covered in this book. We wanted to make you aware of the opportunities and highlight PPC. We also wanted to stress the importance of closely monitoring your PPC campaigns and understanding whether your PPC campaigns are delivering an acceptable return on the marketing dollars you are investing.

When you know the targeted audience you want to reach, PPC is an excellent way to get in front of them.

Ingredient **10**

Email Marketing

A lot of time and money get spent marketing a business to create awareness about your product or service. This generates interest from prospective new customers or potential new patients. When someone is interested in purchasing your product or service, it's called a "lead".

Sometimes your marketing efforts can immediately convert leads into new customers or patients. These customers or patients not only provide new business, they are also an excellent source of repeat business and referrals.

Other times, leads have to be reminded and nurtured before they convert into a new customer or patient for your business. They show interest in your business, but haven't made the decision to "buy".

It's important to routinely communicate with your customers or patients as well as the people mentioned above who may become a new customer or patient.

Email marketing is a very effective tool to do this. It's also inexpensive and efficient. This is one Ingredient you don't want to overlook and many people do overlook this.

Before you can even think about email marketing, you need to have an email database with valid email addresses. So how do you get email addresses to fill your database? Any and every which way you ethically can.
Here is a short list of suggestions:

- Ask new and existing customers / patients for their email addresses.
- Have a website sign-up form where people provide their email addresses.
- Collect email addresses from all website contact submission forms.
- Create unique landing pages for your Pay Per Click Campaigns where name and email address are requested and/or required.
- Collect business cards and email addresses at events.
- Conduct drawings or sweepstakes where people must provide their names and email addresses.
- Give away a special report or ebook in exchange for name and email address. Useful information that gives them something while also serving as a reminder for how you can help them.

- If someone call's your business, ask them for their email address.

What you don't want to do is purchase email addresses or send email marketing campaigns to a database of people who have never even heard of your business, product or service. This practice is not effective and it will more than likely aggravate the people you send it to rather than spark their interest.

These types of unsolicited emails are called SPAM. Most people really don't like SPAM and in the long run, all you will do is hurt the reputation of your business by SPAMMING people. You don't want to be flagged for being spam. If you're sending directly from your own mail server, like Outlook, your email address can actually get blacklisted.

If there is interest in your product or service and someone is willing to provide you with their email address, by all means take it. As outlined above, there is nothing wrong with asking people for their email address or adding email addresses from people who want to be included in your email database.

As you are collecting email addresses, they need to be stored into a database so they are organized, can be easily maintained and are safe. Your email database has value. The more it grows, the more valuable it will get. As outlined above, this is the place to go to and return to time and time again in order to generate new sales and revenues over and over again.

There are a variety of excellent email marketing service subscriptions on the internet that provide you with everything you need to build and maintain your email database as well as to efficiently conduct your email marketing campaigns to that database. The best thing about these on-line email marketing services is they are inexpensive and do not require long term agreements. Here are a few suggestions:

- Constant Contact
- Benchmark
- MailChimp

All of the above are easy to use and have great features. When you create an account on one of these services, you can take advantage of email templates that have already been designed for your email marketing campaigns or you can build your own templates for your campaigns.

When you have an account with one of these email marketing subscription services, everything you create and all the information you enter is safe, secure and organized. It will always be there for as long as you keep your subscription. You don't have to worry about your hard drive crashing, backing up your information or losing an email you've created and would like to use again.

Another great feature about these subscription services is that they offer all types of training, keep you update-to-date on the latest email marketing best practices and keep you compliant with the latest laws and regulations governing email marketing. This includes useful features that allow your recipients to confirm their desire to be a part of your email database or an option to unsubscribe if they wish.

In addition, you will also be provided with tracking and analytical information so you can see how each of your email marketing campaigns is performing. Here's an example of those statistics:

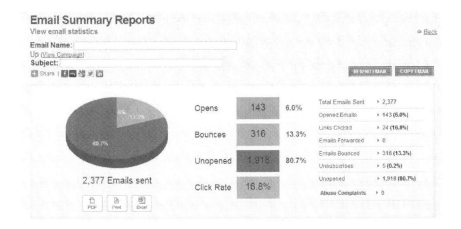

Over time, this data becomes very informative. You will be able to tell what campaigns were most successful. What day or days of the week are most effective for sending your email campaigns? What time of day is most effective for sending campaigns? What messages in the subject line of the email generate the most "opens"?

Use all this information to refine and enhance your campaigns.

So what types of email marketing campaigns should you be sending? That's unique for each business, but here are some suggestions:

- Welcome new customers / patients.
- Useful information about your product or service.
- Special offers or coupons.
- Best wishes for holidays throughout the year.
- New products or services.
- Testimonials from customers or patients.

- Thank existing customers.

Email marketing is an excellent tool to stay top-of-mind in your customers' minds. However, don't overuse this tool. If you send too many emails, people will begin to tune you out. They will "unsubscribe" from your email list and you won't be able to send them future email marketing campaigns. Sending two or three email marketing campaigns per month that are spread out over the month is sufficient for many companies, but some prefer to send out a weekly newsletter. It really depends on how often there is news regarding your company or how often you offer promotions, etc.

Like many of the Ingredients we cover in this book, it takes time, monitoring and adjustments to maximize the potency of email marketing campaigns.

Ingredient 11

Social Media Marketing

Facebook says it has over 1.1 billion users per month. Twitter reports it has over 550 million active users. Google Plus (Google +) states it has over 500 million users currently. LinkedIn says it has more than 200 million users. Pinterest has rapidly grown to over 70 million users.

Social Media is definitely one Ingredient for a winning business marketing recipe. With those types of statistics, it's crazy to ignore these opportunities. However, when it comes to businesses being able to tap into the popularity of these social media sites, it takes a very carefully planned and unique strategy for each of the social media sites you would like to pursue.

Social media sites are rapidly changing and evolving. From a marketing perspective, they offer a great way to reach an audience you would like to target. Furthermore, they allow you to build long term relationships with people who are or may become new customers or patients. If nurtured properly, these relationships can grow to become a very valuable part of your business in terms of loyal fans and a steady stream of referrals.

Based on our experience, if you try to conduct "in-your-face" advertising campaigns on social media sites, you probably won't be successful. That's not what the social media experience is all about and not what these millions and even billions of users want to see. Social media sites are about being "social". That means a focus on people, lifestyles and interaction from a social perspective.

Most businesses that utilize social media sites look at them as an opportunity to directly win over new customers or patients in a short period of time. They begin using social media sites by employing tactics to advertise their product or service just like they would with traditional forms of advertising like print or radio. They may try things like special offers or coupons to get people to act. Over time, these types of tactics can be implemented, but it's generally not a good idea when you are first starting to use social media sites. Normally, it takes a much different and more subtle approach.

Let's outline and discuss methods for starting and growing activity for a business on social media sites along with an overview of the benefits social media sites offer a business.

First let's talk about what advantages social media sites have for search engine optimization (SEO). The major search engines of Google, BING and Yahoo have taken notice of social media sites and are incorporating these social media sites into search engine optimization and search engine functionality.

Google incorporates Google + into its search results. BING does the same thing with Facebook. If the major search engines are paying attention to social media sites, so should you.

Social media sites also provide you with the ability to display your business name, address and telephone numbers. Recall from a previous chapter, this is called NAP and NAP creates a citation on the internet for your business which is another Ingredient for a winning recipe. Remember, make sure your NAP is exactly how it appears everywhere else so you maintain consistency which is essential for SEO. Social media sites also allow you to create a high quality link to your website. Quality inbound links to your website are yet another Ingredient to a winning recipe that can be derived from social media sites.

Based on the above, establishing accounts on social media sites and providing basic information about your business and a link to your website gives you valid reasons to take the time necessary to establish accounts on social media sites.

Now let's talk about the most important reason to utilize social media sites - Getting people to engage with you and share your business with their network of friends.

People buy a product or pay for a service because it fills a need for them. The word "need" is a very broad term. It's always useful to remind yourself of Maslow's hierarchy of needs that you probably learned about somewhere along the course of your education. Here's a diagram of that hierarchy of needs:

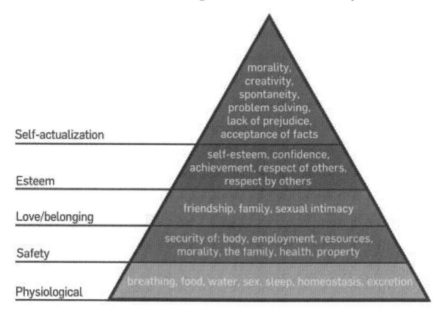

With social media sites, we believe the focus should be on the "Love/Belonging", "Esteem" and "Self-actualization" levels of the hierarchy of needs. You want to connect with people. Invite their input and respect their opinions. When you do these things, people will interact with you and share your posts with their network.

Social media sites are excellent tools to develop friendships, boost the self-esteem of your friends and followers and invite creativity and problem solving. All of these elements are part of the hierarchy of needs as you can see from the diagram.

With all the above in mind, here's an overview of how to start using social media sites that will help your business grow friends and followers that will listen to what you have to say.

"In order to have friends, you must first be one." This is a famous quote from Elbert Hubbard. It's also an important strategy to follow for social media sites. Businesses can have friends and be a friend. You need to think about how you can be that friend. This is something that's unique for every business. It all starts with how your business conducts itself outside the internet as well as how it conducts itself on-line. It's important to be genuine. Based on the above statements, here are some suggestions:

- "Like", "Friend" and "Follow" people on social media sites. When you do this, people will generally do the same for you.
- Make posts about people and their extraordinary stories. For example, maybe one of your customers or patients devotes a lot of their personal time to a charity or perhaps one of them is doing something extraordinary in your community. Just make sure you get the person's consent and permission before making a post about their story on your social media sites.
- Make positive comments about people in your community or the communities where your business is located who are doing good things.

Testimonials about your product or service. There is nothing as powerful as a positive testimonial when marketing a business. People respect and rely on what others think, especially their family and friends. Having customers or patients provide you with a testimonial is a golden opportunity. Testimonials can be used throughout your marketing. Use them in print ads. Put them on your website and post them on your social media sites.

Useful tips and demonstrations. Make posts on your social media sites that provide people with useful tips and demonstrations. The majority of these tips and demonstrations should be about your products or services, but also provide tips and demonstrations about other things. As emphasized previously, don't hard sell your product on your social media sites. Another great idea is to ask your customers or patients for useful tips about your products or services. They see your product or service from a different perspective than you do.

Highlight community events. Be a source for promoting various community events on your social media sites. School sports, art shows, parades, festivals, county fairs and neighborhood garage sales are just a few examples. The list of opportunities goes on and on. If you are a sponsor for these events, make sure to highlight that fact.

Avoid controversy. It goes without saying that you should never make a post on your social media sites that could be considered offensive to anyone or any group of people. Stay away from political issues, religion and other topics that can easily get controversial. You want your business to be respectful of the lifestyles, beliefs and opinions of everyone.

Always ask people. Never miss an opportunity to ask people to "like" or "follow" your business on social media sites. Include this message in print ads, radio ads, billboards, email marketing, website, business card, etc. Most importantly, ask them when they are visiting your store, office or business location.

Boost posts on Facebook. There is a useful feature on Facebook called "Boost Post". This is an inexpensive way to allow the posts you make on Facebook to reach more people. This feature allows you to easily reach the "friends" of your Facebook "friends" (who likely have similar needs and interests), or you can target your posts to a specific geographic area, age group, gender or language.

For as little as $5, your posts can reach a lot of people. If these people like what they see, they will "like" your Facebook page and become a new "friend".

Once you start building "friends" and "followers" on social media sites, it's important to implement tactics that drive them to your website. Here are a few examples of how to do that:

- Post announcements when you add a new blog article to your website with a link to that blog article on your website.
- Post announcements when you add a new page to your website with a link to that page.
- Run a promotion where people have to visit your website to print a coupon. Include the link to your website where they can download the coupon.
- Promote a sweepstakes or giveaway where people have to visit your website to fill out a form to enter the sweepstakes or giveaway. Make sure to include a link directly to the page of your website where they need to go.

Pay Per Click Campaigns on Facebook. Pay Per Click (PPC) campaigns on Facebook can be a very productive tool. When you run PPC on Facebook, you can direct people to either your Facebook page or your website. Generally, we like to direct people to a special landing page on your website where you can capture their contact information, ask them to "like" you on Facebook and provide them with more information about what you are advertising along with a "call to action".

PPC campaigns on Facebook provide you with a variety of options so you can be specific and target the people you want to reach.

Here is a list of options for targeting PPC advertisements on Facebook.

- Geographic region
- Gender
- Age
- Precise Interests
- Family Status (Engaged, Newlyweds, Expecting parents, Parents of children in age groups, etc.)
- Events (birthdays, new job, new relationship, etc.)
- Other types of categories

Special Considerations for LinkedIn. It's important to keep in mind the people you will be reaching on each individual social media site and how you need to communicate with them. A perfect example is LinkedIn. This site is about business, business professionals and careers. Your tactics for LinkedIn should not be the same as the ones for Facebook.

Don't Get Too Automated with Social Media Sites. There are different tools available that allow you to automate your efforts on social media sites. You can link different social media accounts together so when you make a post on one of the social media sites it automatically posts to the other sites. You can also schedule your posts to be delivered on specific dates. For example, you could use one of the automation tools to write 7 different posts all at one time and have each one of the posts added to your social media site on every day of the week. These automation tools can be very handy. However, don't get too automated and routine. People will pick up on that. Keep things fresh.

Follow the basic principles of communication. Communication is not just about delivering messages; it's also about listening and asking questions. When making posts on your social media sites invite comments and questions from your audience. Be sure you are also monitoring your social media sites to respond to questions and comments promptly.

Social media marketing is yet another important Ingredient in your winning recipe. Be sure to use it. Also be aware, social media is an Ingredient that is constantly changing and evolving rapidly. Make sure you are staying up-to-date and changing with it.

Ingredient **12**

Videos and YouTube

Read the book or watch the movie? Most people prefer to watch the movie. Video is a popular Ingredient that will enhance all the other Ingredients we cover in this book.

Once upon a time, producing videos about your business was an extremely expensive project. Even if you did manage to produce a video back when, the best media outlet to utilize your video was an expensive television ad. While high quality video production can still get expensive, YouTube is a great alternative that allows you to create and market videos for free. However, the better quality your video, the more you will stand out."

Let's take a look at why video is an important Ingredient and how it can be used.

Search Engines. Video is another form of content, and search engines like Google, BING and Yahoo love content. Recall that search engines aren't just focused on written content. They love video too! Here's an example of a search on Google using the keyword phrase "Michigan trout fishing"

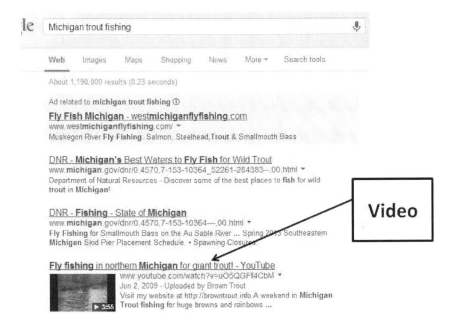

Note how the video is ranked near the top of the search results. You can achieve similar results for videos you produce about your business.

Videos for your website. Including videos on your website is an excellent way to enhance the user experience for people who visit your website. This has a significant impact on conversion rates. Conversions are telephone calls and messages from visitors to your website that are potential new customers or new patients. The increase in conversion rates can be quite high. We have seen video increase conversion rates by as much as 40%.

Videos for your blog. Embedding videos in blog articles is a productive tactic that will enhance your blog. Some businesses even have separate blogs devoted entirely to videos. These are called "video blogs" or "vlogs".

Videos for press releases. Many on-line press release service features provide the ability to link to a video in your press release. That distinguishes your press release and gets it noticed.

Videos for social media sites. Posting videos on social media sites like Facebook, Twitter, Google+ and LinkedIn is an excellent opportunity to engage with your friends and followers. Be sure to ask them to share your videos with their friends and followers.

 Videos for Citation and link building on internet directories. When building the listing for your business on the variety of internet directory sites, your videos should be added to your listing. There are also specific video sites on the internet that allow you to upload your video, input your business information (a citation) and link to your website.

Videos for email marketing campaigns. Each time you produce a video, conduct an email marketing campaign that features the video.

Video Pay Per Click Campaigns. Google Adwords allows you to conduct pay per click campaigns specifically for video. These types of video PPC campaigns can be extremely economical and very effective. When you're running video PPC campaigns, you're taking advantage of the power of YouTube. We will talk more about that in the paragraphs that follow.

Based on the above, you can see the versatility of video, but that's not all. We saved the biggest opportunity for video for last.

In 2006, Google acquired a fast growing video site called YouTube. Google invested a lot in acquiring YouTube (over $1.5 billion) and it has been working hard to get a good return on that investment. YouTube is extremely popular and very powerful. People are conducting searches on YouTube using keyword phrases much like they do on Google. YouTube is an opportunity you don't want to ignore.

You should establish a YouTube Channel for your business. This is yet another opportunity to create a citation for your business as well as link to your website. Upload your videos to your YouTube Channel and make sure your videos are optimized for searches. That means having appropriate titles for each video, writing descriptions for each video, and creating tags for each video that are relevant to the content of the applicable video.

When you set-up your YouTube Channel, it should have a distinctive image just like TV Channels do. When you think of NBC, ABC, ESPN, FOX, CBS, DISCOVERY and FOOD NETWORK, they all have unique brands. While you don't have to get as sophisticated as these major TV networks, think about ways to set yourself apart on your YouTube Channel much like they do.

The most exciting thing about YouTube is that it is relatively young. Its full power and potential is yet to be seen. Make sure you are positioned to take advantage of what YouTube has to offer both now and in the future. We are confident your efforts to include YouTube will be a good short term decision and an even better long term one.

Ingredient **13**

Go Mobile

The exact number depends on what study or report you read, but around 91% of American adults have a cell phone or smart phone. Ninety-one percent!

If you aren't already, get familiar with the word "mobile". It's where the internet and internet based marketing are headed. It's going there very fast.

Everything we have covered in this book related to the internet has a mobile version or a mobile "app" (application). The popularity of smart phones and tablets require that you provide users with a "mobile friendly" experience. Otherwise, they are likely to move on to a competitor who does.

It all starts with a mobile version of your website or a mobile responsive design. These versions are specifically formatted to fit the small screen of a mobile device. Having your website accommodate mobile devices makes it easier to use. If you didn't have a mobile website, a visitor using a smart phone will probably find your website cumbersome, difficult to read and hard to navigate. When a website is troublesome to read and use, visitors will leave and move on.

Here's an example of a mobile website using a fictitious company, XYZ Auto Parts:

Note how the mobile website fits within the small screen of the smart phone. Also note how simple and easy to read it is.

Another important design element to note in the above mobile website example is how it keeps navigation choices to a minimum. It displays only the most vital information for a mobile user. In this case, the location, offers and how to contact the business are the most important menu items. When you have a mobile version of your website, you most likely will not want to duplicate all the information from your desktop website.

The search engines are another reason to go mobile. A search conducted on Google using a mobile device is not the same as searching on Google at your desktop computer. Remember that Google, BING, Yahoo and other search engines are trying to make it easy for their users. If Google knows you are using a smart phone to conduct a search on Google (and they know), it wants to give you the best experience and the highest quality results possible. That means it will give you search results that accommodate mobile use.

Text messaging or "texting" is yet another reason. Texting is a very popular form of communication. Texting is not just about connecting with your family and friends. It's also a way for your business to communicate with customers or patients as well as *potential* customers or patients.

We could take every Ingredient listed in this book and talk about how mobile use is influencing that Ingredient. However, we don't think we need to do that.

Simply put, if you are not taking advantage of mobile opportunities today, you are missing out on new customers or patients. If you don't move into the world of mobile soon, you will be at a huge disadvantage. It's that important.

A mobile version of your website doesn't have to break the bank. There are many options that will allow you to create a mobile version of your website at a very affordable cost.

If you haven't gone mobile when it comes to marketing your business, go now!

Ingredient **14**

Direct Mail

It's very important to be diversified in your marketing. In order to maximize your marketing reach, you cannot rely solely on the internet. As you may remember, we touched on this subject in a previous chapter when we talked about press releases.

Marketing off-line is as critical to your success as marketing on-line. An effective off-line Ingredient that you should consider is direct mail. This is especially useful if you need to target people in a very specific geographical region.

Prior to the internet becoming an effective marketing tool, direct mail pieces flooded mailboxes. At least half the mail received daily was from a variety of different businesses. That isn't the case anymore. Therefore, there is a lot of opportunity today to get your business noticed in the mailboxes of people you would like to reach. What is old has become new again.

If you won't take our word for it, you might like to know that a big user of direct mail campaigns is Google. That should tell you something when an internet giant is using direct mail.

Direct mail can get expensive and time consuming. In a typical direct mail campaign, you will have costs associated with:

- Design of a direct mail piece
- Printing
- Acquiring names and addresses for a mailing list
- Postage

Because of the time and cost, direct mail is not something most small businesses incorporate into their marketing. However, there's a great option offered by the United States Postal Service (USPS) that makes direct mail campaigns affordable and efficient.

Every Door Direct Mail or EDDM is a unique program developed by the USPS. It allows you to create a direct mail program on the USPS website (**www.usps.com**) that has the following features:

- Ability to select the specific geographical area where the direct mail campaign is going to be sent.
- Ability to select whether you want to mail to businesses or residences.

- No mailing lists are necessary. You do NOT need individual names and addresses.
- No postage meter necessary.
- Pay for the postage on-line at the usps.com website using a credit card.
- All necessary documents that need to be submitted with your direct mail pieces to the post office(s) are automatically generated and can be printed from the USPS website.
- Discount postage prices. (currently the price is sixteen cents ($0.16) per piece – that is subject to change)

Here's what the USPS Every Door Direct Mail website looks like:

As you can see it's not complicated.

There are also options available on the USPS website that allows you to find a local printer (if you don't already have one) as well as someone to design your direct mail piece.

To read all the details and requirements of the USPS Every Door Direct Mail Program, visit usps.com and select the menu item for "Business Solutions". You will see a drop-down menu and an option for "Try Every Door Direct Mail".

One of the best things about the EDDM program is the customer support provided by the USPS. If you have a question or need help, your telephone call or email to the USPS EDDM support staff is answered promptly. When we first started using the EDDM program, we had questions and needed feedback to make sure we were following the proper procedures. The USPS EDDM customer service representatives were friendly and helpful. Our telephone calls were taken right away and our email messages received a reply within 24 hours.

We've used EDDM for clients and the results have been good. It all starts with a carefully designed direct mail piece that gets noticed and delivers messages and special offers that compel people to act.

Here's an example of a direct mail campaign using the EDDM program for the fictitious company we created in a previous chapter – XYZ Auto Parts:

XYZ Auto Parts just opened a new store on the west side of Toledo. They would like to announce the grand opening to people who live in residential neighborhoods within a 3 mile radius of the new store.

An oversized post card direct mail piece was designed with a size that measured 7" in width by 12" in length (7 x 12). A post card of that size complies with the USPS EDDM requirements and gets noticed in the mail.

The final design of the post card looked like this:

Using the EDDM tool on the USPS website, the marketing manager at XYZ Auto Parts input the store's address and selected all residential addresses within a 5 mile radius. The EDDM on-line tool showed the manager there were 4,873 residential addresses within the 5 mile radius. All 4,873 addresses were selected and a total postage cost of $774.88 was calculated. The marketing manger provided an expected drop-off date of the mail pieces to the post office and then selected the "pay on-line" option. After entering the company's credit card information, the transaction was complete and the required documentation to be submitted with the mail pieces was automatically generated and printed. Everything for the direct mail campaign related to the post office was now complete except for dropping off the pieces at the post office for delivery.

The marketing manager called the company's local printer who quoted a printing estimate of $1,169 for the 4,873 oversized post cards. The marketing manager accepted the estimate and authorized the printer to proceed with the order. Five days later the print order was complete.

The marketing manager took the direct mail pieces and the required USPS documents to the post office location listed on the documents and gave everything to the USPS employee at the customer service counter. The next day the USPS mail carriers for the designated routes were delivering the direct mail pieces to all the residential households within a 5 mile radius from the new XYZ Auto Parts store.

The total cost of the mail campaign was:

Post card design - $250.00
Printing - $1,169
Postage - $774.88

Total = $2,193.88 or $0.45 per piece.

Two weeks after the direct mail campaign had been launched a report showed the marketing manager that 584 coupons had been used from the mail campaign post cards which resulted in sales that totaled $27,192. In addition to the sales, the direct mail piece provided a steady stream of traffic to the new store in its first two weeks of operation.

While the above is only an example, we've conducted direct mail campaigns for clients with excellent results using the Every Door Direct Mail program. It is definitely a useful tool and can be an essential Ingredient for successfully marketing your business.

Ingredient **15**

Print and Classified Ads

Contrary to popular belief, print advertising is not dead. They are still printing newspapers, magazines and other publications. More importantly, people are still reading them. That's why print advertising should not be ignored. It deserves a portion of your marketing budget and it is a vital Ingredient for a winning recipe in marketing your business.

We concede that print advertising isn't the dominant force it used to be. The internet has played a huge part in knocking print advertising off its throne.

It's important to be as targeted as possible with your print advertising campaigns and look for opportunities that don't cost a lot of money. Here are some suggestions for economical and efficient print advertising campaigns:

Community / Neighborhood Publications.

Almost all major newspapers have opportunities to advertise in geographically specific locations. If your business is located in a major city, we are talking about special editions or special sections of newspapers that focus on the community or neighborhood where your business is located. Using these types of community-specific publications, you are going to reach people who are located in close proximity to your business. Convenience for customers or patients plays a big part in their decision-buying process.

Industry-Specific and Interest-Specific Publications.

It's surprising how many industry-specific and interest-specific publications are available. Most of these have a very loyal readership. If your business has customers or patients located within a specific industry or with specific interests (and you do), there are targeted opportunities to reach these people. For example, let's assume your business is a law firm in Pennsylvania that has a big portion of your practice focused on legal issues associated with the oil and gas industry. There are many publications devoted strictly to oil & gas. There are also publications focused on large land owners such as farmers who own the land where energy companies want to drill.

Classified Ads.

Yes, the classifieds ads in newspapers and magazines are advertising opportunities that are underutilized. To effectively utilize classified ads, you need to determine who you want to reach so you can get highly targeted with your ads. Using the example of the Pennsylvania law firm from above, a classified ad in the "Land Acreage For Sale or For Lease" section of the classified ads would reach the right audience.

The following is a list of tips to remember when preparing a print ad:

- Keep your ad simple and straight forward. Less is more.
- One big headline message. Keep it short.
- One small sub-headline message. Can be longer than the main headline but still keep it concise.
- Not too much written copy.
- Use high quality and high resolution photography that compliments your written messages.
- Always display your telephone number and website address.
- Always use your logo for branding purposes.
- Always use a call to action – "Call Now" or "Hurry, Limited Time Only"
- Don't cram every detail about your business in the ad so it looks cluttered.
- When using full color ads, keep the colors clean and pleasing to the eye. Limit the use of colors to just 2 or 3 different colors.
- If possible, include a coupon (with an expiration date) in the print ad for a special offer – it's a great way to track the response from the campaign.

Here are two examples of print advertisements. Which one do you think is better?

Not everyone relies on the internet to search and find products and services. If you're not taking advantage of highly targeted and cost effective print advertising opportunities, your business may not be reaching all its potential customers or patients.

Don't forget about this Ingredient. Formulating your winning recipe of Ingredients depends on it.

Ingredient **16**

Events

Most businesses understand the importance of sponsoring and participating in community events. It's great for public relations and it gets your business exposure. But that's not all.

This Ingredient is much more comprehensive and versatile than you might expect. When you add this Ingredient to your winning recipe, it mixes wonderfully with all your other Ingredients and takes them to another level.

There are all kinds of opportunities to sponsor and participate in events where your business is located. Here are just a few:

- Chamber of Commerce
- Parades
- Festivals
- Charities
- Little Leagues
- School Fundraisers
- Marathons, 5K Runs, 10K Runs, etc.
- Gun Shows
- County Fairs
- Art Shows
- Home Shows
- Boat Shows
- Holiday Toy Drives

You will find the list of event opportunities either in your community or near the community where your business is located goes on and on when you start to do some research. Be selective and target the events that will benefit your business.

You don't have to participate in every event. When you read the list below of how an event can be used in your marketing mix, you may feel that you don't have the time, but you really should take part in at least two or three events throughout the year.

Here's a list of how just ONE event will benefit your business prior to the event, during the event and after the event:

- Create an "Events" page for your website. Shows website visitors your involvement in the community where your business is located. It also helps to keep your website "fresh" by updating it with new content. *(Ingredients 1 and 3)*

• Organizations who organize events usually will have a website. You can have information about your business and a link to your website on that organization's website. This creates both a citation and an in-bound link to your website which is great for SEO or search engine optimization. *(Ingredients 4, 5 and 6)*

• Prior to the event, it makes for a good press release from your business both on-line and off-line. Talk about your sponsorship of the event and what it's all about. Distribute the press release to local newspapers and publications as well as submit to on-line press release services. *(Ingredient 8)*

• Create an email marketing campaign announcing the upcoming event and "eblast" it to your database of email addresses. *(Ingredient 10)*

• Write a blog article about the event, it's history, how it benefits the community and your sponsorship. *(Ingredient 7)*

• Make posts about the event on the social media pages for your business *(Ingredient 11)*

• Create a direct mail piece for the event that invites people to the event and an opportunity to receive a special offer when they stop by your booth or table at the event. *(Ingredient 14)*

- Feature the event in a print advertisement. Create a coupon with a special offer that ties into the event. *(Ingredient 15)*

- Set-up a booth or table at the event. You and employees of your business who are comfortable interacting with the public should be stationed at the table. Go out of your way to talk and interact with people. Be cheerful, friendly and inviting! There is nothing like meeting people, shaking their hands, looking them in the eye and talking with them genuinely. They will remember you and your business.

- Hand-out brochures at the event.

- Have a drawing for prizes at the event. Require people to fill out a card with their name and email address in order to enter the drawing. Add the email addresses collected to your email database.

- Giveaway an inexpensive promotional item at the event. Make sure that promotional item has your business name, logo, tag line, telephone number and website address clearly listed. For example, pens are a great advertising promotional gift. Promotional pens are inexpensive and something people will actually use and are less likely to toss in the trash.

- Make sure you and your employees who attend the event give out your business cards to people you talk to. Also make sure to collect business cards from people.

- Take photographs during the event.

- Send a thank you card to people you talked to at the event. Include a special offer for them if they visit your business.

- Send an email marketing campaign specifically to the email addresses you collected at the event. Include a special offer for your business. *(Ingredient 10)*

- Write a press release about the event and submit the press release both on-line and off-line with a couple of photos you took during the event. *(Ingredient 8)*

- Post photos taken during the event on the social media sites for your business. *(Ingredient 11)*

- Write a blog about the event and post it along with photos taken during the event. *(Ingredient 7)*

- Send an email marketing campaign that includes your event photos to your database of email addresses. *(Ingredient 10)*

As you can see, you get a lot of mileage from your event sponsorship and participation. Make a video during the event and you can add even more Ingredients to the mix.

For the reasons listed above and many others, it's difficult to find opportunities that market and promote your business and allow you to interact with the public in the same way that community events offer. They are a critical Ingredient for success.

Ingredient **17**

Analytical Tools
(Google Analytics, Google Webmaster and More)

We've covered sixteen different Ingredients prior to this one. If mixed properly, they will help you create a winning recipe for your business. So, how do you know if you have the proper amounts of these Ingredients and whether or not they are working? What's the measuring cup?

The answer is there are all types of measuring cups to utilize. These are known as analytical tools. They are an important Ingredient that will provide you with a wide variety of valuable information. Once you have this valuable information, you will then be able to use it to your marketing advantage.

We are going to highlight the benefits of two very important tools: **Google Analytics** and **Google Webmaster Tools.** We are also going to briefly cover some other useful analytics tools.

Google Analytics

Google Analytics (**http://www.google.com/analytics/**) provides a wealth of information about your on-line activities. It's a free service, but the information you can obtain from Google Analytics is priceless.

To get Google Analytics, you need to sign up for a Google Analytics account. Once you establish an account and provide your website information, it will generate a tracking code that must be placed on your website. Once that tracking code is in place and working properly, all types of wonderful information will start to show up in your Google Analytics account.

These are the types of general answers that can be answered with the information provided by your Google Analytics account:

- How many visits did my website receive this month?
- How many of these visits were from different visitors (unique visits)?
- How much time did these visitors spend on my website?
- What pages of the website did they visit?
- How many of these visitors to my website were new visitors vs. returning visitors?
- Where are the people who visited my website located geographically?

- How many people access my website using a desktop computer vs. a mobile device?
- How many visits are generated by my Pay Per Click Campaigns (PPC)?
- What blog articles have been the most popular?
- How many visits to my website do I have this month compared to last month or to the same month last year?
- Are the pages of my website engaging people?
- What's the behavior of visitors to my website?
- Where is the traffic from my website coming from?
- What impact do my social media accounts have on my website traffic?
- What search engines drive traffic to my website?
- What keywords did people use to find my website?
- Which pages of my website have the highest bounce rate? Can that page of the website be improved so it's more engaging?

If you can think of a question about your website, chances are Google Analytics will have the information needed to answer that question. It's that powerful.

Let's look at an example. You want to know how your website is generally performing. When you access your Google Analytics account, you are provided with the following overview:

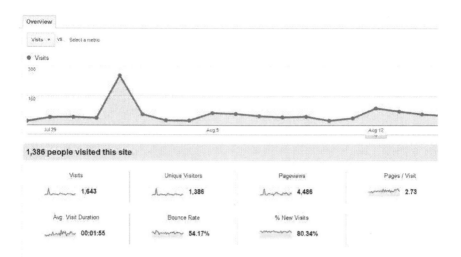

As you can see, Google Analytics tells you the total number of visits. It shows how many of those visits were unique. It provides information about the average amount of time visitors spent on your website and how many different pages they looked at on average. It's extremely valuable data that provides you with the critical information you need to determine if your Ingredients are creating a winning recipe.

Let's review some of the high level metrics in more detail:

Visits: As the name implies, this is the total number of visits to your website for a defined period of time. If the same visitor visited the site today and also visited the website tomorrow. It would count both of those visits from the same visitors. Therefore, this number counts duplicate visits.

Unique Visitors: This is the number of unduplicated visitors to your website. A unique visitor is only counted once.

Average Visit Duration: This is the average amount of time visitors spend on your website. Generally, anything over 2 minutes is good. Obviously, you want to keep people on your website as long as possible so they learn about your business and absorb your messages. The longer a visitor stays on your site, the higher the probability they will convert to a lead (contact your business).

Pages Per Visit: This is the average number of your website's pages a visitor visits. Typically, anything over 2 pages is good. You want a visitor to visit as many pages on your website as possible so they learn more about your business.

Bounce Rate: This is a percentage that tells you the number of single page visits to your website. When a visitor lands on one page of your website, they don't go any further and visit more pages. They leave after seeing that one page. You don't want them to do that. You want them to dig deeper, spend more time on your website and visit multiple pages. While there are exceptions, if you have an overall bounce rate of less than 50%, it's good.

You should look at the statistics of individual pages of your website and determine exactly what pages visitors are arriving to your website on. The page of your website where a visitor enters your website is called an entrance page. For the most part, people arrive at your website on your Home Page, but they could also arrive at some other page. In fact, the more targeted you get with your website, the more you will see a variety of different pages that are entrance pages. Some pages will have higher Bounce Rates than others. You should regularly take a look and see what pages have over a 50% Bounce Rate so you can determine what enhancements need to be made to improve the Bounce Rate.

% New Visits: This metric tells you what percentages of your visits are visiting your website for the first time. You want a steady stream of new visitors, but you also want visitors coming back to your website. You should think of ways to generate both new visits as well as repeat visits. A good rule of thumb is the 50/50 rule - 50% returning and 50% new visits. However, these percentages can and will fluctuate based on your type of business and industry.

You also want to know where visitors to your website are located. Google Analytics has data that will answer that question. This can be useful for a variety of reasons.

If your business has only one store in one city (let's say Toledo) and you are generating traffic to your website from all over the United States, you may need to think about what you can do to get more targeted and specific to your market.

This information may also identify opportunities for expansion. Let's assume you have a store on the south side of Toledo, but you notice from your Google Analytics data that a lot of visitors to your site are coming from the north end of Toledo. This may be an indicator that you should open a store on the north end of Toledo to serve those people and expand your market share.

Here's an example of the information that can be obtained from Google Analytics regarding the location of the visitors to your website:

Google Analytics first provides information by country:

Country / Territory	Visits (?)	↓
	2,240	
	% of Total: 100.00% (2,240)	
1. United States		2,149
2. Canada		12
3. United Kingdom		10
4. India		9
5. Philippines		9
6. Japan		6

Then you can drill down and get more detailed information. If you click on "United States" you can see data for individual states:

Region	Visits (?)	↓
	2,149	
	% of Total: 95.94% (2,240)	
1. Ohio		1,323
2. California		76
3. Florida		72
4. New York		60
5. Texas		59
6. Pennsylvania		51
7. Illinois		47

You can once again drill down to get even more details by city:

City	Visits ?	↓
	1,323	
	% of Total: 59.06% (2,240)	
1. Akron		205
2. Ottawa		139
3. Columbus		135
4. Cleveland		72
5. Canton		44
6. Cincinnati		38
7. Cuyahoga Falls		27
8. Parma		27
9. Medina		21
10. Toledo		20

Another useful piece of information you can gather from Google Analytics are the sources of the traffic to your website. It will answer questions like this:

- What traffic is coming from Google searches?
- How many visits from Pay Per Click?
- Are people coming to the website from email marketing campaigns or a particular email marketing campaign?
- Do any of the citations created for my business generate visits to my website?
- Does Facebook send visits to my website?
- Did the press release I submitted send visits to my website?

All these types of questions can be answered with Google Analytics. Here's an example that shows visits to a website coming from a variety of sources including Google, Yahoo, BING, an email marketing campaign and more:

Source / Medium	Visits	↓
	1,673	
	% of Total: 100.00% (1,673)	
1. google / organic	993	
2. (direct) / (none)	284	
3. yahoo / organic	99	
4. bing / organic	94	
5. visitor.benchmarkemail.com / referral	44	
6. google.com / referral	27	
7. yellowpages.com / referral	23	
8. aol / organic	16	

In this book, we are merely scratching the surface of Google Analytics and what it can do for your business. It's worth taking the time to visit the Google Analytics website to learn more about this productive tool.

The best decisions are informed decisions, and Google Analytics can help you make good, informed decisions that will greatly benefit your business and enhance your marketing efforts.

Google Webmaster Tools

Google Webmaster Tools (**www.google.com/webmasters/tools/**) is another account you want to establish for your website. Google Webmaster Tools shows you information about how Google crawls your website, whether or not it encountered any errors that need to be fixed and how it indexes the pages of the website. It also provides you with information about internal and external links to your website as well as the keyword searches that were used to find your website.

Here are examples of that information:

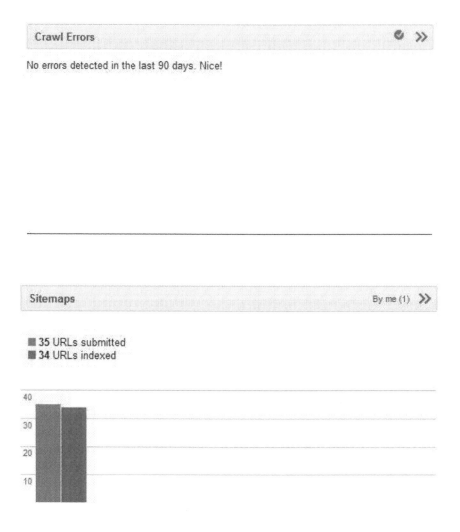

Google Analytics and Google Webmaster can and should be linked together to optimize the information generated by both tools.

The above is not your only source for analytical information. A lot of the Ingredients we have covered in this book also have analytics features.

Google Adwords (Pay Per Click)

Monitoring the performance of your Pay Per Click (PPC) campaigns is critical to your success with PPC. If you don't frequently monitor, PPC can get very expensive and unproductive. The analytical information provided by Google Adwords allows you to easily monitor the performance of your PPC campaigns.

Google Adwords can and should be linked to your Google Analytics account. The information contained within Google Adwords will provide you with each campaign's activity. You will be able to see how many clicks to your website, total cost, what position your ads maintain on average and how many conversions (leads) you receive from your PPC campaigns on Adwords.

Using the information supplied by Google Adwords along with Google Analytics, you will be able to quickly make adjustments in your campaigns and determine if they are either beneficial to your marketing efforts or too expensive to be feasible.

Here's an example of the Google Adwords Analytical information:

Clicks [?]	Impr. [?]	CTR [?]	Avg. CPC [?]	Cost [?]	Avg. Pos. [?]	Conv. (1-per-click) [?]	Cost / conv. (1-per-click) [?]
29	1,950	1.49%	$5.86	$169.89	2.9	0	$0.00
0	0	0.00%	$0.00	$0.00	0.0	0	$0.00
0	0	0.00%	$0.00	$0.00	0.0	0	$0.00
134	17,207	0.78%	$5.73	$768.08	2.2	26	$29.54
0	0	0.00%	$0.00	$0.00	0.0	0	$0.00
0	0	0.00%	$0.00	$0.00	0.0	0	$0.00
0	0	0.00%	$0.00	$0.00	0.0	0	$0.00
0	0	0.00%	$0.00	$0.00	0.0	0	$0.00
58	1,358	4.27%	$4.42	$256.33	1.9	4	$64.08
227	43,044	0.53%	$1.12	$253.90	1.3	0	$0.00
448	63,559	0.70%	$3.23	$1,448.20	1.6	30	$48.27

Similar type of analytical information can obtained for Pay Per Click Campaigns you run on BING / Yahoo.

Whatever Ingredients you use in your winning recipe always looks for the analytical information that is provided with that Ingredient. Without the wealth of information provided by all these tools, it will be very difficult to formulate your winning recipe. With them, you will be equipped and prepared to create a winning recipe that only gets better over time.

Taste Testing, Evaluation and Recipe Refinement

The National Food Management Services Institute has a standardized recipe evaluation form for measuring recipe success. Here are their five (5) traits to rate a recipe:

- ✓ The appearance of the food
- ✓ The taste of the food
- ✓ The temperature of the food
- ✓ The texture of the food
- ✓ The overall acceptability of the food

A winning recipe is one that has been tested, evaluated and refined until it reaches a level of success. The recipe for successfully marketing your business isn't much different.

A recipe is a mix of ingredients. There are all sorts of recipes that never amount to anything because they were just thrown together. A winning recipe is a special mix of ingredients that has been tested, evaluated and refined over time.

Make sure you have a system in place to test, evaluate and refine your recipe. Every business is different and so is every winning recipe. The mix or the amount of each Ingredient is going to be unique for your business.

The group of people who "taste" your recipe and provide feedback should be employees as well as customers or patients. Remember, the way you think your recipe of Ingredients "tastes" may be different than what your potential new customers or patients think about the taste. It's vitally important to make that first impression, that "first taste", the very best it can be."

Expect to make changes to Ingredients. Some of the changes will be subtle. Others will be more substantial. Make those Ingredient changes, stir and have them "tasted" again. Over time and with persistence, you will find your ideal blend of Ingredients that produces your winning recipe.

Maintaining the Consistency of Your Recipe

Winning recipes maintain their consistency. Taco Bell tacos and McDonald's hamburgers taste the same in California as they do in Maine.

Just like those successful fast food restaurants, you should maintain the consistency of your winning recipe. That starts with being:

1. Relevant
2. Authentic
3. An Authority

You may recall these *Three Important Words* from the beginning of this book. Adhere to those three words and your chances for success will increase dramatically.

Consistency is also important for branding your business. Over time, branding becomes more powerful and more valuable. While we all can't brand our businesses globally like Apple, Microsoft, Nike, Coca-Cola and Google, you can brand your business in your marketplace. Your marketplace could be a big geographical region or a small one. Regardless, branding your business is an integral part of your long-term success.

Maintaining the consistency of your recipe and nurturing your brand comes from all departments of a company, not just the marketing department. Teach everyone in your organization the recipe and the importance of following it. When everyone internally understands and maintains the consistency of your recipe, its distinctiveness will come through externally. Potential customers and patients will see why your product or your service is different from your competition.

Sous-Chefs
Finding the Right Help

Any good chef has sous-chefs backing him or her up. These sous-chefs make sure the winning recipe gets executed to perfection time after time. The sous-chefs may not get all the glory and fame, but without them, the chef and the restaurant would not be successful.

Your business needs sous-chefs to help you develop your winning recipe. These sous-chefs may be employees and/or they may be outside consultants, contractors or services. No matter what form they take, your sous-chefs must understand your winning recipe. They must also recognize the significance of each Ingredient and how that Ingredient mixes with other

Ingredients to create a winning recipe. That means effective communication and training on your part.

There are all types of outside services that you can engage to handle one or many of the Ingredients we have outlined in this book. Like any type of service, there are good ones and there are not so good ones. Here are three tips to keep in mind when considering engaging outside services:

Avoid long term commitments.

It's a good rule of thumb to avoid signing long term contracts with anyone or any business you would like to help you with your Ingredients. In our experience, long term agreements lead to complacency. Services get placed on "auto-pilot" and that's unproductive, especially in an environment like the internet where change is constant. Short term agreements or month-to-month agreements are are advisable and in your best interest. Make those who you engage earn your continued business each and every month.

This doesn't necessarily mean making changes to your consultants, contractors and other service providers. It simply means put yourself in a position that fosters performance and results on a monthly basis. If you are getting the results, keep them engaged. If not, then terminate them and find someone better.

When you do find someone good and they are consistently performing for you, it pays to have them with you on a long term basis. The more they get to know your business and understand your winning recipe of Ingredients, the more effective they will be for you.

Beware of promises.

We see a lot of people make promises like: "We will get your business and your website to the top of Google." The fact of the matter is no one can make that promise (except Google). If you want to hire people to help you with your website and SEO (search engine optimization), the good ones will tell you they can't make any guarantees that you will be ranked at the top of Google. However, these are usually the types of people who will get you there. They know how to do things right but they are straight forward and honest with you.

Ask to see sample portfolio of work.

You should always ask to see a portfolio of work. When that portfolio is provided, the work typically speaks for itself in terms of quality, creativity and professionalism.

Check references.

It's always a good idea to check references. You do it when you hire an employee. You should do the same thing if you are hiring a consultant, contractor or other outside service. Don't just check the references that are provided to you. Also do some research yourself and check references that you find.

If it hasn't been already, your business will be bombarded by people and companies soliciting you for your business. They can waste a lot of your time with false claims and empty promises. Do your homework before engaging them and make sure you are not tied down by a long-term commitment that will be a major headache if you need to get out.

These simple tips will help you avoid wasting time and money.

We hope you are successful with developing your winning recipe using the Ingredients we have discussed in this book. Keep in mind a winning recipe isn't limited by the list of Ingredients we have talked about. There may and probably will be other ingredients you want to add along the way. Your business is always evolving. Your recipe should too.

Authors

 Tom Liebrecht

Tom Liebrecht is the President and Managing Partner of Marketing Quarterback Consulting. A marketing and business consulting firm he founded in 2008.

Prior to starting Marketing Quarterback Consulting, Tom held vice president positions for regional and national real estate development companies where he was responsible for acquiring, building and marketing large scale, mixed-use master planned communities.

Over his 25+ year career, Tom has gained a wealth of experience and a reputation for producing positive results using a mix of business fundamentals, creativity and an uncanny ability to recognize untapped opportunities.

Tom and his team provide a wide variety of consulting and outsourcing services to all types of businesses in a variety of industries.

He and his team have helped clients implement the Ingredients contained within this book that created winning recipes.

To contact Tom and learn more about Marketing Quarterback Consulting, please visit **www.marketingQBC.com**

Bill Kozdron

LuckyFish Media, created and managed by Bill Kozdron, is a website design company specializing in Wordpress Web Design, Online Marketing and Website Management. With experience both as a professional video producer, videographer and website designer for the past 15 years, Bill's diverse technology oriented background gives him the perfect mix of creativity and business sense that aids businesses in attaining an online presence that is both unique and effective.

Though he has an IT degree, Bill is constantly adding to his repertoire of skills, staying on top of new website and marketing trends. In an environment that is constantly evolving, Bill's continuous search for knowledge gives clients a real advantage, which is vital for any successful web presence to maintain their competitive edge.

His primary areas of professional expertise include:

- Website Design
- WordPress Design and Theme Modification
- Professional Web Training via Video
- SEO research and planning
- Social Media Planning and Marketing
- WordPress Website Maintenance
- Online Marketing
- Professional Videography
- Video Editing (Adobe Premiere and Avid)
- Video Production

Bill has an IT Degree focusing on Project Management from Capella University in Minnesota as well as an Associates Degree from Lansing Community College. Bill completed his IT degree while working full time as a professional video producer.

Bill was born and raised in Michigan and currently lives in Williamston with his wife of 12 years and his 10 year old son. He enjoys golfing, playing video games with his son & spending time with his wonderful wife, Sheri. In addition, Bill has yet to find a situation in life that he can't relate to golf.

To learn more about Bill's professional services, visit **www.LuckyFishMedia.com**.

25735607R00093

Made in the USA
Charleston, SC
13 January 2014